SURVIVAL KIT

By
G. Brent Darnell

This book is dedicated to all of the tough guys in this world who make things happen.

Front cover photo by **Fred S. Gerlich Photography**
Back cover photo by **MK Coppola**
Cover design and layout by **Tudor Maier**

Other books by **G. Brent Darnell**

The People Profit Connection, How Emotional Intelligence Can Maximize People Skills and Maximize Your Profits

Communication and Presentation Skills for Tough Guys

Relationship Skills for Tough Guys: 12 Steps to Great Relationships

Stress Management, Time Management, and Life Balance for Tough Guys: Creating Success on Your Terms

The Primal Safety Coloring Book

The Tao of Emotional Intelligence: 82 Ways to Improve Your Social Competence

Big Mama's Country Cookbook: Recipes from the True South

Table of Contents:

Communication and Presentation Skills

Relationship Skills

Stress Management, Time Management, and Life Balance

COMMUNICATION AND PRESENTATION SKILLS

By
G. Brent Darnell

Introduction

This book was written for tough guys. And make no mistake. The term "guy" is not gender specific. You know who you are. You are the ones who get things done. You are the alphas, the ones who make things happen, the grease that keeps things moving. You are the ones with calluses on your hands and mud on your boots. You are the tough guys. But did you know that same get-r-done attitude that you possess may be holding you back in some ways. How can that be possible?

Think of someone you look up to, someone you admire, a mentor, a leader in your field. Think of someone who is the best of the best. Now ask yourself, "What makes this person who they are? What are the characteristics that make this person the best of the best?" You will likely come up with a long list of characteristics. They are passionate and assertive. They make people feel special. They have great relationship skills, a sense of humor, a drive. It is always a list of the so called "soft" skills. But there is nothing soft about soft skills. It's what makes us who we are. And it is those soft skills that separate the great from the good. You need these soft skills to be successful.

That is my business, teaching soft skills to tough guys using something called emotional intelligence. Emotional intelligence can be defined as social competence or the ability to deal with people. I mostly work with construction folks and engineers. When I told my wife that I was going to teach emotional intelligence to technical people, she laughed. How could I teach these folks all of these soft skills that I know they needed to become successful? Even I had my doubts. How would they react to learning about their own emotions and the emotions of others? The initial reactions, which are now predictable, were apprehension, skepticism, and resistance. But once these initial reactions were overcome, and participants realized that emotional intelligence was something that could be quite important for their career development and personal lives, virtually all of them embraced the concept. And once they embraced the concept and worked on their emotional intelligence, the results were nothing short of remarkable.

This book is all about communication and presentation skills, an area where most tough guys do not excel. Part 1 is a 12-step process that, if followed, will give you great confidence and will allow you to communicate effectively with just about anyone. Part 2 is about presentation skills and the ability to get up and speak in front of any audience. And as most of you know, communicating your ideas and motivating others is the key to success. How many of you are not comfortable speaking in front of a crowd? How many of you freeze up when you have to carry on a conversation with a stranger? This book will give you the confidence to be able to master both of those with ease.

Part 1
12 Steps to Great Communication

Why are tough guys poor communicators? We have done much work with tough guys, and there is actually a typical emotional profile that most tough guys have that prevent them from being great communicators. They tend to have high self-regard, assertiveness, and independence, but fairly low emotional self-awareness, empathy, social responsibility, and relationship skills. This is a recipe for communication disaster. They tend to be poor listeners and come across as aggressive and somewhat dismissive. So how do we fix that? With a 12-step method to improve your communication skills.

Step 1: Listen, listen, listen.

Keep your mouth shut and listen to what people are saying. Don't just hear the words, understand the words. Use paraphrase listening. Repeat what they say in your own words to be sure you understood them. Tell them, "So what you're saying is . . .". God gave us one mouth and two ears. Your question to statement ratio should be two to one. If you are talking too much, close your mouth. You will be amazed at how this works. For those of you who are nervous about talking to people that you have just met, and you feel like you don't have anything to say, just try to get them to talk about themselves. Generally, people love to talk about themselves, especially men. Once you get them talking, you will find that it will be hard to get a word in. And at the end of the conversation, they will probably tell others what a great conversationalist you are. And you made that impression by saying nothing.

Step 2: Verify your understanding.

We do an exercise where you get a partner and think of a popular song that everyone would know like an anniversary song or anthem. Then each person taps out their song on the table and the other person tries to guess the song. Prior to this exercise, they think that this will be quite easy. But as it turns out, they get the right song less than half the time. Why is that? In your mind the song, such as Happy Birthday, is so clear in your mind. Why doesn't this other person get it?

Communication doesn't happen until each person has an understanding of what the other person is communicating. This takes verification. You can't verify enough. Ask questions and verify the information. Offer to verify your own information. Say it several different ways and ask the person what they heard.

Step 3: Increase your vocabulary.

You can sign up for emails that send you a new word each day. Keep a dictionary and thesaurus handy and use them often. There is a thesaurus in Word so that you can make different word choices. Don't go overboard on this. Don't use a long word when a short one will do, but in general, a better command of the English language will help you be more precise and more persuasive with your communication.

Step 4: Find the best ways to communicate.

If you want to be a good communicator, practice the following forms of communication in order, the most effective to least effective:

> Face-to-face
> Video conference
> Telephone
> Voicemail
> Written (email, text message, letters, memos)

A word on emails. Emails are probably one of the worst forms of communication there is. But we tend to use it way too much. Why is it so ineffective? Because communication is as much as 95% non-verbal. Most of what you convey to others is through body language, facial expressions, and tone of voice. So you are only working with a miniscule percentage of your communication. How many times does email get misconstrued because there is no way to tell where the emphasis is, there is no way to tell if they are being ironic. If the communication is important, ditch the email and either meet the other person or pick up the phone and call them.

Email is no different than any other communication. Be nice. Use please and thank you. Don't write in CAPITAL LETTERS or **BOLD LETTERS** because it means you are **SHOUTING AT THE PERSON!** If appropriate, write on your email that there is no need to send a reply or thank you. Don't forward emails to long lists of people. If you want to forward something to an individual because you think they might enjoy it, that is courteous, but don't overdo it.

If you want to put the best face on your email and increase the chances of someone actually reading it, try the following:

1. Put something interesting in the subject line. If possible, put your entire message in the subject line.

2. If you cannot put the entire message in the subject line, make the email short enough so they can read the entire email without scrolling down.

3. Don't add attachments unless absolutely necessary or if an attachment is expected.

People will appreciate this cyber courtesy. In addition, there is a greater probability that your emails will actually be read.

Let me share with you an email I received from a company where I purchased something online: "We're just checking in to see if you received your order from Better World Books. If your order hasn't blessed your mailbox just yet, heads are gonna roll in the Mishawaka warehouse! Seriously though, if you haven't received your order or are less than 108.8% satisfied, please reply to this message. Let us know what we can do to flabbergast you with service. Thanks again for your support! Humbly Yours, Indaba (our super-cool email robot)"

Now that is a cool email that is read and appreciated.

A word on writing letters: The same thing for emails holds true for letters. You are only conveying a small percentage of the communication, so make it short, sweet, and to the point. Keep it simple and use concrete language. Don't tell jokes and don't use irony.

Step 5: Keep an eye on body language and facial expressions.

If you are not sure what you are conveying, you may be conveying something you don't want to convey. Tough guys, in general, have low emotional self-awareness. If you are one of those guys, I encourage you to take an acting class or a dance class to develop some body awareness.

Know what your face is conveying at all times. For most tough guys, their face is much too serious. This is fine if you are delivering a eulogy, but for true open, honest communication, open your face up to some expression.

Also pay attention to other's facial expressions and body language. Use your empathy skills and make adjustments based on their reaction to you. Keep in mind that most tough guys score low in empathy, so this may take some work.

Step 6: Challenge your mental models.

We all have something called mental models. An example of mental models is the following riddle. You are going through the woods and you see a cabin in the woods. You open the door, walk in, and find that everyone is seated in rows and they are all dead. How did they die? Try a few guesses. Give up? It's the cabin of an airplane. You had the mental model of a log cabin, and no matter how you tried to reason, that mental model prevented you from coming up with the right answer.

We all have these mental models, and many times, it is not conducive to good communication. We have models about other people, other professions, and future encounters with others. The trick is to have the awareness to understand when you are projecting a mental model and challenge it. When you do away with mental models, you open yourself up for open, honest communication.

Always project the best outcome. Your energy going into a situation can affect the outcome. So if you go in with a negative attitude, you will likely come out with a negative result.

Step 7: Don't climb up the ladder of inference.

There is something that many of us do often. It's called the ladder of inference. We take information and draw conclusions that may be right or wrong. These conclusions lead to other conclusions that become facts, and before you know it, you have reached a totally erroneous conclusion. One example: A person is late for one meeting, so you assume that he will be late for all meetings. This leads to the conclusion that he is always late. This further leads to the conclusion that he is not a team player. Then you keep climbing up the ladder and decide that he should be fired. So how did you get here? You climbed up this ladder and are prepared to fire this person. How do you climb back down the ladder? By challenging your assumptions, asking questions, and verifying the information. Why not ask this person why he was late for a meeting? He may have a very good reason. Always challenge and verify and stay off the ladder!

Step 8: Avoid destructive communication.

When you participate in gossip, when you tear people down, it not only hurts them, it hurts you. Don't tolerate gossip and negative talk about others. Try to find the good in others and build them up. Gossip can destroy communication and relationships. It creates negative energy that is conveyed whether you are aware of it or not. Make a commitment right now.

Step 9: Use the language of diplomacy.

Unless you are working on your assertiveness or need very clear communication, it is wise to use qualifiers where appropriate. Avoid absolutes like don't, can't, never, or always unless very clear communication is needed. Try to use these instead:

Could be, might be, may have, would be . . .
A bit, a slight, a short, or so, a little . . .
I'm afraid, I'm sorry, I prefer . . .
Not (very) convenient . . .
I was wondering, if it's not too much trouble- . . .
With respect, to be honest, to put it bluntly . . .
"Would like" instead of "need"

Step 10: Avoid communication killers.

Try this experiment. Ask someone a question that starts with "why". Then ask them for the same information by using who, what, when, where, or how. Ask them if they feel the difference. Why questions sound like interrogations. They feel like accusations. Avoid them and see if this creates a better dialogue with the person sitting across from you.

Avoid "yes, buts", "yes, howevers", or "no buts", especially if someone is bringing you an idea. It will kill the communication. Marshall Goldsmith has an exercise in his book, *What Got You Here Won't Get You There*. It's called Pay it Forward. You solicit advice from others, and they give it to you. Instead of saying, "I tried it and it didn't work", or "that won't work" or "that's a stupid idea" all you say is, "Thank you." Get used to saying thank you when others bring you ideas. It will maintain the relationship and keep the communication flowing.

Step 11: Use voicemail wisely.

Voice mail can be a good way to communicate. Keep in mind that it is the first impression many people have of you, so make your outgoing message interesting, maybe a little humorous. Smile, speak clearly and distinctly, and make it short. Check your own outgoing message right now or have someone check it for you and give you their impression. And when leaving voicemails, make them short and to the point. Make it clear when no callback is needed. Don't just say your name and then tell the person to call you back. If possible, convey the information you want to convey if it doesn't take up too much time. Always leave your number because not everyone carries your number in their head or in their phone.

Step 12: Avoid the use of I and me.

Try this exercise. Ask someone to tell you a problem and then try to have a discussion with them without using the words "I" or "me". It is quite difficult for some. Many of us are problem solvers and we want to show how smart we are by telling them, "Here is what I would do." I never knew how much I used the word "I" until a friend of mine from Argentina pointed out that I used the word "I" eleven times in a short email. I didn't believe him, but when I went back and looked, it was true. Even though I wasn't trying to do it, the email sounded very arrogant. Have you counted the number of "I"s in this paragraph? Be conscious of how much you use this. Go on a break from talking about yourself or using the words "I" or "me" for a day and see how it goes. This will really open up your communication with others.

Part 2
Presentation Skills and Rhetoric

As most of you know, speaking in front of an audience is difficult. In fact, in terms of our greatest fears, speaking in front of an audience is always listed near the top. For many, speaking in front of people is a stronger fear than death. Jerry Seinfeld put it this way: "Most people would rather be in the casket than have to stand up and give a eulogy." This is especially true for tough guys.

I am a mechanical engineer by training, but at one point in my career, I quit engineering and became a full-time actor for three years. My claim to fame was a small role on *In the Heat of the Night* in which I played a redneck auto mechanic drug dealer. After three years of struggling to become a full-time actor, I resumed my career as an engineer, but I took some wonderful things with me from my training as an actor. Acting helped me to be more comfortable in front of audiences and with people in general.

While facilitating a management development program for a multi-national company, I hired a professor from the Massachusetts Institute of Technology, one of the most prestigious schools in the country, to teach a segment on rhetoric. He had multiple degrees including a PhD, and he had published hundreds of articles and several books on rhetoric. I talked with him on the phone, and he sounded pleasant and articulate.

He began his presentation by putting a transparency on the overhead projector. The transparency was a typed page, single spaced, with very small type. This professor said "Uh" every third syllable. His voice cracked. To make matters worse, he leaned against the table on which the overhead projector sat and jiggled his leg. This shook the image that was already difficult to read.

Then it hit me how brilliant this man was! He was doing all the things that we should never do. What a great way to teach! The only problem was that he kept going. I finally realized that he was not acting. This was his presentation. I stopped him and took a break. I frankly told him the problems with the presentation. He apologized and vowed to correct his mistakes, but when he resumed his presentation, he did it exactly the same way. I ended up dismissing him and teaching the segment myself.

This experience made me realize that no matter how much you know about a subject, the way you present is vital in order to communicate your message. This is especially true for the tough guy engineers and construction folks that I work with. They think that if you give the audience enough information, if you inundate them with data, if you put up a lot of complicated graphs on PowerPoint and show them specific areas with a laser pointer, they will be wowed. This is simply not true. The message is not in the slides. It's in the presentation. And presentations can be very powerful without any visual media. People will be persuaded by you during a job interview or a project presentation because they like and trust you and make a connection with you. The information you are conveying is secondary to that.

I have taken the concepts I learned as an actor and applied them to public speaking and presentation. I hope that it will help you to overcome your fears, even if you believe that you are not proficient at speaking in front of an audience. If you already do well with public speaking there may be some things in this book that will help you, give you a different perspective, or give you a new way to approach your presentations.

Think of your presentation as a theatrical production, a stage play if you will. If you are an actor playing a role, then it is much easier to allow yourself to be creative in your approach to presenting. If you prepare as an actor prepares, using the following guidelines, your presentation should be markedly better, perhaps even spectacular. And you may even receive that actor's dream: a standing ovation from the audience.

I have also included a section that covers a simplified version of rhetoric, the ancient art of persuasion. This will help you to formulate better arguments and motivate your audience to action.

The Production:

A theatrical production has many components that work together to create a unique experience for the audience. Many of these components are the same for presentations. When you create a performance, you tell a story with drama or comedy or both. You move the story along with imagination and emotion. You motivate your audience and shape their reactions based on what is happening on stage. When you do a presentation, you should strive to do the same thing. I have listed a few of these theatrical characteristics below:

• Audience
• Character
• Costume
• Body, Voice and Movement
• Script
• Set
• Props
• Technical stuff: lighting, sound and music
• Rehearsals
• Opening Night
• Rhetoric

The Audience:

You must know your audience well. Ask the following questions: Who is your audience? Are they from another country or culture? What is your audience's education level? Have you used any words that they may not understand? Will they understand you if you speak too quickly or use idioms or jargon? Does your audience possess the technical skill that you possess? What are you trying to convey to them? What motivates them? What barriers exist between you and the audience? What do you want to say? What do you want to achieve?

Once you have asked these questions, you will know your audience better and make any necessary adjustments to your speech. There are too many examples where native English speakers speak far too quickly and use local idioms while addressing international audiences. The audience is lost within the first five minutes. We engineers tend to get caught up in the delivery of information: technical terms, facts, and figures. This can be boring for a technical audience and a total disaster for a non-technical audience. The audience will "check out" five minutes into the speech. See the section on rhetoric for more information on tailoring your message to match the audience.

Character:

Whether you know it or not, you play a character when you speak in front of an audience. Are you the boss, the expert, the specialist, or perhaps, the consultant? Ask the following questions: What is your status? Is it high, medium, or low? What role are you playing for the audience? How do you want them to perceive you? This will give you clues as to how to present yourself. Do you want to be the guy from the outside with all the answers or perhaps just one of the guys talking to them as if it were a casual chat?

Costume:

Dress appropriately for your audience. Ask the following questions: Should your dress be casual/dressy/a costume? What are your audience's expectations? Do you want to meet their expectations or throw them off by wearing something completely different?

Dress appropriately for the message. If you are delivering a humorous message, a humorous costume may be appropriate. If you are delivering a message on how to dress for success, blue jeans or overalls probably wouldn't make much of an impression unless you were making an opposite point. Surprises can be fun.

I was giving a presentation to the sales staff at a resort located in a small town south of Atlanta. Since I arrived in the town early, I decided to eat breakfast in a local diner. I met a man at the door. When he saw me in a suit and tie, he exclaimed, "A suit and tie in Pine Mountain. You must be either a preacher or a bill collector." It made me realize I was overdressed for this presentation. I took my tie off and unbuttoned the top button of my shirt.

When I worked for a large contractor in Atlanta, we were presenting to a school board in a small, South Georgia County. We all arrived in our suits and ties. Many on the school board were dressed very casually. One of them, a local farmer, wore overalls. We did our fancy, citified presentation on PowerPoint with a projector. Needless to say, we did not win the project. We would have been much better off if we had dressed casually and presented the information on poster board.

What you wear says much about you and your message. Dress appropriately.

Body, Voice and Movement:

Body/Face:

Be aware of your body language at all times. Some people are naturally stiff in their body language. You can see it around their shoulders and neck. For those stiff body language types, some physical warm-up exercises may help. Try to loosen up before a presentation. Do some stretches and try to relax your body. You may be a sloucher. If you are, be aware of it and try to hold your shoulders back and your head up. If you don't you may come across as uninterested or apologetic.

Do you have nervous ticks and gestures? Be aware of what your body is doing or you may convey to the audience nervousness, ineptitude, or boredom. If you're not sure, you may want to video tape yourself and study it prior to your presentation. Be sure to separate your speech and your movements. Don't try to move while you are speaking unless it is for effect. Move, set yourself, then start talking. Smile if it is appropriate to the message and use facial expressions. Don't have a stone face.

One last note about your face. Ask yourself the following: What does your face convey when you are not trying to convey anything in particular? If you are unsure, ask someone close to you. I pointed out to one of my clients that he had an angry face. He said that his children approach him all the time and ask him if he is angry. This surprises him each time. He is not an angry person, but he has an angry face.

Do you have a serious face? A bored face? A sad face? Does that look fit with your message? I once watched a presenter with a sad face try to motivate a crowd and convey unbridled enthusiasm, but his face would not let him. If your face does not convey your message, then you must work on it. Practice in the mirror. Are you conveying the right expression to your audience at all times? Spouses and trusted colleagues are good resources for this. Ask them to let you know what your face is conveying.

Voice:

If you have to constantly clear your throat, it can be quite distracting. Do a vocal warm-up. A good vocal warm-up is making a buzzing sound with your lips, opening and closing your mouth while making sound and massaging your face while making sound. Vary the pitch and tempo of your voice. Avoid monotone. Articulate. You must be understood. Speak slowly and distinctly. Use pauses effectively. Pause . . . for . . . effect. Practice your pauses. Write them in if necessary.

Second Languages:

I have found that presentation skills have very little to do with language. I have taught these skills to Swedish and Spanish speaking participants. They presented in English. When they began to struggle, they wanted to switch to their native language. After the switch, the presentation was exactly the same, only in their native language. Communication is up to 95% body language, voice intonation, and non-verbal cues. So don't get too wrapped up in language.

Accents:

If you have a regional accent or an accent from another language, the audience will make assumptions about you that you may or may not want. For instance, in the US, if someone with a deep, Southern accent talks in front of an audience from the North, they tend to make assumptions about this speaker, that he is uneducated and dim witted. For this reason, you may want to consider diminishing or eliminating your accent. It takes time, but it can be done.

I was born in Mobile, Alabama, and had a very strong Southern accent growing up. When I became a full-time actor, I decided to get rid of my accent or be doomed only to play Southern roles. I bought a tape recorder, recorded my voice, listened to it carefully, and worked to eliminate my accent.

A word . . . um . . . about . . . uh . . . uttering . . . uh . . . um:

If you are "um"ing and "uh"ing your way through your presentations, this can be a major distraction to the audience. It can make you come across as hesitant, uninformed, and unprepared. You may not even realize how much you are doing it. This is not a difficult thing to improve upon. Use a video tape or audio tape during your rehearsals to see where these gems lie. You can also have a friend correct you. Some speakers groups ring a small bell whenever these halting words are said. However you do it, get rid of the "um"s and "uh"s. If you um and uh, the audience will think you are inept. If you use silent pauses, they will think you are brilliant.

Movement:

Move with ease and grace. Be confident. Try to be fluid and relaxed. Use gestures. Don't deliver a speech with your hands at your sides. Practice gestures so that they are natural and effective. Practice and work on your proprioception, which is the sense of knowing where your body is in space. We do a warm-up exercise where we all walk across the room with the centers of our bodies in different places. We put the center in our heads and are transformed into cerebral nerds. Then we put the centers in our chests and become tough men. Then, it's the hips and we are all runway models. Then, we try something different. I ask the group to imagine themselves as the CEO of a large company walking into a stadium filled with employees. How would you feel? What message would you send? Remember, the way you walk into a room and up to the podium will give the audience impressions which can add to or detract from what you are trying to say.

If you want to learn how to effectively use your body for incredibly motivating presentations, I would recommend that you study evangelist preachers or rock-and-roll stars. You don't have to emulate them exactly, and you should always develop your own style to fit your personality, but these folks really know how translate their body language into crowd motivation.

Don't let your movement get in the way of a good presentation. Don't try to do too many things at once. Sometimes, presenters try to talk, move and change slides at the same time. Remember this rule: **Do one thing at a time.**

A few tips on body, voice, and movement:

Take a few deep breaths before your presentation to relax. Have room temperature (not cold) water available in case you have a dry throat. Don't drink or eat any dairy products before speaking. They may coat your throat or cause mucous, which may cause problems. Attach an emotion to whatever you are saying. That emotion may change throughout the presentation, but it should be a conscious choice. Visualize what you are thinking. If you have visual aids, this is a bonus, but even if you don't you must be able to see what you are trying to convey in your mind's eye. If you can see it, your audience will be able to see it.

Script:

Try not to read your presentation. It is better to miss a few things and try to connect with the audience than to look down the whole time reading from a piece of paper. Learn your lines and then have the confidence to speak from your heart, not from the page. Any time you relay a personal story, you should tell it. When you read a personal story, you come across as insincere.

Set:

Ask the following questions: How is the room laid out? Is it adequate? Should the stage be elevated for better sight lines from the audience? Where are you to stand? Can you be seen by everyone? Is there a podium? Do you need one? Are there any distractions you should be aware of such as local train whistles, announcements over public address systems, bright lights through a window, air conditioning systems going on and off? Where is your audience going to sit? Will you be able to address them properly? Check for any power cords and other trip hazards. Check the location of all tables, podiums, AV equipment, etc. If you need to, relocate them so that you can move without having to think about these potential obstacles.

After you ask these questions, you will be better equipped to make some adjustments to make your presentation even better.

Props:

Props can be very effective metaphors. Are there things besides PowerPoint slides to show the audience? A picture or physical representation speaks volumes. Do you have a model or a tangible, three dimensional illustration? Use the props effectively. Either show it early for effect or bring it out as a surprise. For an environmental presentation, we showed a physical representation of how much trash our company generates per year. We showed how the trash would fill 1,000 Olympic sized swimming pools. This was a much more effective way of presenting the information than reciting the number of cubic yards.

Technical Stuff: Lighting, Sound and Music:

The technical side of a presentation is only noticed when it doesn't work. This is something that is commonly overlooked.

Check all audio visuals before your presentation. Make sure everything is working properly: overhead projectors, LCD projectors, microphones, flip charts, white boards, markers, etc. LCD projectors are getting better and better, but older models sometimes have problems with compatibility to laptop computers. Always have alternatives just in case.

Microphones:

Learn a little bit about mike techniques. When you are at a podium mike, make sure you don't move your head around too much or your audience will hear uneven sound. Levelor mikes are great inventions, but make sure the placement is good or your sound will be uneven. It is very annoying when speakers rub their Levelor mikes or tap them with their hands. The sound is annoying and the presentation becomes all about the speaker rubbing the microphone.

If your audio visual technicians are really sophisticated, you may have a monitor so you will hear what the audience hears. If you have this, you can make adjustments as necessary. Do a microphone check prior to your presentation if possible. You may also test to make sure you can be heard in the back. Ask someone to sit in the back prior to the presentation and make sure you can be heard. Don't ask the audience if they can hear you. This may convey to them that you are not prepared.

You will want to prepare your presentation in several formats in case there is a problem. Have it on a thumb drive, but you should also be able to do the presentation without anything. It is better to be prepared. Make sure you are properly lit and make sure you can see your presentation on the podium if there is one.

For flip chart presentations, make sure you have plenty of flip chart paper and make sure your markers are not dry. Also make sure your white board is clean and has a good eraser and that your white board markers are not dry. When you write on a flip chart or white board, make sure you write large enough for everyone to read, even in the back of the room.

PowerPoint slides:

Most presentations can be done without PowerPoint. Many people use it as a crutch. There are also alternative like Prezi as well as some great Mac applications. But too many audio visuals may prevent you from truly connecting with the audience. I try to use PowerPoint only for visuals, graphs, and videos (things I can't convey as well by talking). By the way, be careful about embedded videos. They will not save to a new file if you transfer the PowerPoint to your laptop. You must re-insert the video. Be sure to check volume and size of the video prior to your presentation to make sure they can be seen and heard.

If you must use PowerPoint, don't make your slides too busy. Too many photos and visual images can be overwhelming to an audience. Don't overdo the fly-ins, dissolves and sound effects. If overused, they can distract from the message. Keep it simple. If you must use words on a slide, use bullet points. Use as large a font as possible and bold them if you can. They should be very easy to read. Try to use no more than five words per line. Use action verbs instead of passive language. If a bullet point says "increasing the bottom line", change it to "**INCREASE THE BOTTOM LINE!**". Cartoons and jokes are always a good way to get your point across if they pertain to the message. Pay attention to your audience and make sure your jokes don't offend.

Don't read your slides. The Audience can read. Give them a few seconds to read the slide, then begin speaking. Don't talk while you are advancing slides. Perform the action, then speak. Don't stand in front of your slides. For an LCD projector, point to the projected image on the wall if you need to emphasize something. I personally don't like the use of laser pointers and find them to be annoying.

Try to have some music playing beforehand. Have you ever watched a movie without sound? It's rather boring, isn't it? The same principle applies for people walking into a large, empty room. If the room is silent, the energy is low. This is not a good way to start. I encourage you to have some type of music playing as the audience enters the room. Choose the music to match the mood of your presentation. If you are trying to motivate the audience, choose motivating music. Imagine coming into the room with the theme from Rocky playing in the background. It tends to pump people up and prepare them for your presentation. Prior to a session on the company's environmental initiatives, we had songs like *"It's not Easy Being Green"* and *"What's going on?"* playing in the background. It set the proper mood for the presentation.

Rehearsals:

Practice your presentation, but don't over-rehearse to the point where it has lost its energy. Be confident. Find the time to practice until you are comfortable. Video tape your presentation and watch it to improve your performance.

If you are having trouble with your presentation, try these tips to practice:

1. Give your presentation as if you were giving it to a group of five-year-old children.

2. Sit down and practice your presentation. This will allow you to focus on your delivery and content without having to think about all of the other elements. Once you have practiced while sitting, try it standing up as if you were in front of an audience.

Technical Rehearsals:

Be sure to take the time to rehearse how to work your audio visual equipment such laptop computers, LCD projectors, white boards, etc. You should use these items with grace and ease. If your slides have links to websites, make sure you have an internet connection.

Final Dress Rehearsal:

Try to run through one last time prior to your performance using as many of the elements as possible. This should bring out any problems, weaknesses, and areas that may need a little tweaking and improvement. Directors give actors "notes" after their rehearsals to improve their performances. Find someone you trust and ask them to give you feedback on your presentations.

Opening night:

You are finally ready for opening night, your magnificent performance, your world premiere. If you have prepared properly, opening night is nothing but fun. Take a few deep breaths and let yourself be a little nervous. This will keep you on your toes and give you some energy. Enjoy yourself and have the confidence to know that your presentation will WOW your audience.

Rhetoric: a systematic approach to creating persuasive arguments.

Introduction and Thesis: State what you will accomplish or what your argument is. It may be good to start out with a question. Example: "What are we going to accomplish in the coming year?"

Main Points (Argumentation): State 2-3 main points to support your argument.   Example: "We're going to increase sales, reduce overhead without eliminating jobs and increase our bottom line."

Some types of arguments:

General to specific: Everyone is tightening their belts because we don't know when the economy will turn around. We should do the same.

Specific to general: We're tightening our belts at home. Our subcontractors and vendors are tightening their belts. Our competitors are tightening their belts. Every company on the planet is tightening their belts and reducing costs.

Convince using threats: If we don't tighten our belts, we are going to have to lay off a lot of people and face the possibility of going out of business.

Always arrange your argumentation from the weakest to the strongest. End on the strongest. You can also include opposite arguments in your arguments. If you know that someone will be opposing your argument, you can say, "I know that some of you think that belt tightening creates fear and uncertainty. But I believe that by being honest with our present situation and working together, we can get through these tough times."

Conclusion: restate your premise and draw a conclusion. Motivate the audience to action or convince them that your argument is sound. Example: "If we work hard and accomplish these three things, it will also increase our bonus pool and profit sharing."

Rhetorical devices:

Metaphor: This is a device that uses comparison for a stark image that the audience can relate to immediately. Jesus used these frequently in his many parables. Example: We need to make cuts without losing an arm and a leg.

Simile: Comparison using like or as. Example: Not tightening our belts would be like putting a gun to our heads.

Rhetorical question: Example: How many of you want to be looking for a new job? If we don't tighten our belts, that may be the case.

Ethos, Pathos, Logos: These are three basic methods to convince an audience. You must know your audience and choose the right approaches. You may use one, two or all three.

Ethos. This is the ethical argument. Appeal to the audience's sense of right and wrong. Tell them "It's the right thing to do."

Pathos. This is the emotional argument. Appeal to the audience's emotions. One example is when we are shown photographs of starving children. This appeals to our emotions and motivates us to action.

Logos. This is the logical argument. When you are dealing with technical people such as scientists and engineers, appeal to their logical side. Give them the facts and figures. Tell them "If we reduce our accidents by 5%, our insurance costs will decrease by 15%."

If you choose the wrong approach, the results could be disastrous. If you choose pathos for a group of PhD physicists, your message may not be understood. Using the example of the school board in the small South Georgia County, we tried to give them a very logical approach to building their school, but in the end, we know we should have used more pathos. The decision for them wasn't based on logic, but emotions.

There is one other vital device to use during a presentation: storytelling. Tell an impactful story that will elicit an emotional response from your audience and they will never forget what you say. I'll give you an example.

I do this as a way to show people how weak PowerPoint can be. I show a slide with too many words, giving the audience some statistics on social networking, how many million people log onto Facebook every day, trying to show them the reach and power of social networks. Then I continue with my presentation.

That's when I get into storytelling. I tell them a story of a young couple whose child was dying of leukemia and they were looking for a marrow donor. In desperation, they posted their plea on Facebook and found a donor. I know of someone who found a job using Linked In. And in the Middle East, there is a revolution taking place being fueled by Facebook and Twitter. Now those are amazing examples of how powerful social networking can be.

At the end of the day, I ask them if they can remember anything from the PowerPoint slide on social networking. They remember very little. Then I ask them if they remember the stories I told about social networking. They remember them all in detail.

Thoughts and tips:

- Believe in what you are saying. Make it more than just information.

- Speak from the heart.

- Make eye contact throughout your presentation.

- Be sincere.

- Be energetic. Use gestures.

- Avoid monotone. Vary the pitch and volume of your voice.

- Read and acknowledge the situation. Adjust if necessary. Be flexible. If there is a noise in the room or a big moth flying around the stage, don't just press on. Acknowledge the problem, make a joke about it, deal with it, then move on.

- Concentrate and focus. It may help to do a short preparatory meditation before your presentation to increase your focus and concentration. A few rounds of deep breathing can relax you and focus your energy.

- Rehearse: practice to a level that you feel comfortable, but don't memorize or over-rehearse. It's good to be a little bit nervous. It can keep your energy up.

- If you are nervous, it is likely that you are focusing on yourself. Take away that focus and put it on the audience and your message.

Tips:

- Triptychs are effective!
  "Friends, Romans, countrymen . . ."
  "I came, I saw, I conquered."
  "of the people, by the people, and for the people"

- Repetition can be effective.
  Martin Luther King's "I have a dream" speech.

Another example is John F. Kennedy's inaugural speech. Here is an excerpt. Note the repetition of "let both sides".

"Let both sides explore what problems unite us instead of belaboring those problems which divide us. Let both sides, for the first time, formulate serious and precise proposals for the inspection and control of arms—and bring the absolute power to destroy other nations under the absolute control of all nations. Let both sides seek to invoke the wonders of science instead of its terrors. Together let us explore the stars, conquer the deserts, eradicate disease, tap the ocean depths, and encourage the arts and commerce. Let both sides unite to heed in all corners of the earth the command of Isaiah—to "undo the heavy burdens ... and to let the oppressed go free.""

- Silence . . . can be . . . . very . . . effective. Work on your pauses and don't rush through your presentation. And if you get stuck, use the pause to gather your thoughts.

Get some support:

There are many speaking classes and speaking groups and clubs. If you are serious about improving your technique, take a class or join one of many speaking clubs such as Toastmasters *www.toastmasters.org*. The members will give you feedback and pointers on your presentations.

To recap the process:

1. **Audience**: Know your audience.

2. **Character**: Know what role you are playing.

3. **Costume**: Dress appropriately for the audience.

4. **Body, Voice and Movement**: Watch your body language. Know what you are conveying at all times. Do a vocal warm-up. Be aware of your type of face and make the necessary adjustments.

5. **Script**: Know your material, but don't read or memorize word for word.

6. **Set**: Check out the stage beforehand.

7. **Props**: Use visual examples and powerful metaphors.

8. **Technical stuff**: lighting, sound and music: Check out all audio visual equipment prior to presenting if possible.

9. **Rehearsals**: Practice and get feedback from trusted colleagues.

10. **Opening Night**: Relax, take some deep breaths and focus. Be enthusiastic and energetic. Believe in what you are saying.

11. **Rhetoric**: Use the ancient art of rhetoric to motivate the audience to action.

A final word:

I wish you the best of luck in your presentations and hope that this book has helped you in your quest to become a better speaker. Keep in mind, this is a process. The more you present, the better you will become, so be kind to yourself, especially in the beginning. As they say in the theatrical world, break a leg!

RELATIONSHIP SKILLS

12 Steps to Great Relationships

By
G. Brent Darnell

 **Introduction**

This book was written for tough guys. And make no mistake. The term "guy" is not gender specific. You know who you are. You are the ones who get things done. You are the alphas, the ones who make things happen, the grease that keeps things moving. You are the ones with calluses on your hands and mud on your boots. You are the tough guys. But did you know that same get-r-done attitude that you possess may be holding you back in some ways. How can that be possible?

Think of someone you look up to, someone you admire, a mentor, a leader in your field. Think of someone who is the best of the best. Now ask yourself, "What makes this person who they are?" What are the characteristics that make this person the best of the best? You will likely come up with a long list of characteristics. They are passionate and assertive. They make people feel special. They have great relationship skills, a sense of humor, a drive. It is always a list of the so called "soft" skills. But there is nothing soft about soft skills. It's what makes us who we are. And it is those soft skills that separate the great from the good. You need these soft skills to be successful.

That is my business, teaching soft skills to tough guys using something called emotional intelligence. Emotional intelligence can be defined as social competence or the ability to deal with people. I mostly work with construction folks and engineers. When I told my wife that I was going to teach emotional intelligence to technical people, she laughed. How could I teach these folks all of these soft skills that I know they needed to become successful? Even I had my doubts. How would they react to learning about their own emotions and the emotions of others? The initial reactions, which are now predictable, were apprehension, skepticism, and resistance. But once these initial reactions were overcome, and participants realized that emotional intelligence was something that could be quite important for their career development and personal lives, virtually all of them embraced the concept. And once they embraced the concept and worked on their emotional intelligence, the results were nothing short of remarkable.

This book is all about relationships, something that many tough guys struggle with. There is a step-by-step process that, if followed, will give you great confidence and will allow you to establish and maintain great relationships with just about anyone. And as most of you know, having great relationships is the key to success. Relationships give you ideas, encouragement, and opportunities. It drives business and your personal success.

How many of you are uncomfortable at parties, gatherings, and networking events? This book will give you the confidence to be able to master those situations with ease. Part 1 is the 12 steps to great relationships. Part 2 is common courtesy, which is the foundation for all great relationships both business and personal. I discuss the tools to use, the situations you will encounter, and the chain of courtesy. I will give you practical information that you can readily apply so that you will become a master of relationships.

Part 1

12 Steps to Great Relationships

Part 1
12 Steps to Great Relationships

12 Steps to Great Relationships

n Africa, they have philosophy known as Ubuntu. When you greet someone, you say, "I see you." They answer by saying, "I am here." In other words, you don't exist until the other person acknowledges you. Imagine the implications of walking past someone in the office because you are pre-occupied. You are, in essence, saying that they don't exist. There is a sense of being connected to every other human being. I think we've lost that sense of being connected to each other, and relationships are all about those connections.

In our classes, we show the first scene from the movie, *The Godfather*. In it, Bonasera, the funeral director, asks the Godfather to kill some guys who beat up his only daughter. The Godfather's response at first is no. Why does he refuse him? Because, as the Godfather says, "You don't ask with respect. You don't offer friendship." Bonasera had not cultivated a relationship with the Godfather prior to asking him for a favor. How many times do we do that on construction projects? We don't cultivate relationships with other stakeholders. Then, we need something from them. Is it any wonder that more times than not, they refuse to cooperate?

The following twelve steps will help you establish and maintain great relationships. There is nothing magic about these twelve steps. You may have more steps or less steps. Apply them to your life and work as you see fit.

Step 1: Know yourself, develop yourself and become more self-aware.

As tough guys, we tend to shun away from self-knowledge. We're just too busy getting things done. But the first step toward great relationships is getting to know yourself better. Generally, tough guys have low emotional self-awareness. Partly, it's just the way our brains are wired. That, plus society has told us, especially males, that we should not let our feelings show. We are not supposed to recognize or share those feelings, so we have a tendency to shut ourselves down.

In order to be good with others, you must first explore yourself. There are many ways to do this. The first thing I recommend is to build in some kind of reflection time each day. We tough guys have a tendency to spend about 80% of our time and energy at work and the other 20% on our family. Have you done the math yet? That leaves zero time for ourselves. This must change if you are to become more self-aware. Look for ways to explore who you are, what you are about. This reflection time is crucial for your personal development. You cannot spend this time working, planning, or strategizing. You must use it for total reflection.

Sit down in a quiet place and just reflect and be. We are human BEINGS, not human DOINGS. Most tough guys have this insane notion that you must constantly be DOING something. And by adopting this attitude, you rarely find the time to just BE. Find the time before the family gets up or after they go to bed. But find the time. It is vital for your well-being and success.

There are more ways to tap into who you are. During this reflective time, you can meditate or be prayerful. You can explore your values. You can become more aware and involve all of your senses. Sit quietly and note what you see, smell, hear, touch, and taste (if you are eating or drinking at the time). You don't have to set aside time to become more aware. You can practice something called mindfulness. That's where you are fully present and in the moment all of the time. There have been studies done on mindfulness, and it actually decreases stress levels. It is also great for relationships because when you are with someone, you are fully present with them, and that makes them feel important.

If you want to know more about mindfulness, check out any book by Jon Kabat Zinn. He teaches mindfulness to executives. If you don't have the time or inclination to practice mindfulness, you can always do it at meals. We tend to rush through our meals without fully experiencing the sights, sounds, textures, and taste of the food.

I recommend taking courses in self-discovery. There are also some great books on the subject. Peter Senge's *The Fifth Discipline* is one. Stephen Covey's *7 Habits of Highly Effective People* is another. Take the EQi (emotional intelligence evaluation) or a personality test so that you can know yourself better. These evaluations will give you clues as to your strengths and weaknesses. Fully explore who you are, and you have taken the first step toward great relationships.

Be relentless in your thirst for knowledge about yourself. Always look for ways to improve. Know your strengths and weaknesses. Try to develop the areas that are holding you back. This self-knowledge is the foundation for all great relationships.

Step 2: Develop a genuine love or at least acceptance of yourself

Be comfortable with yourself. Accept yourself with all of your limitations.

This may be hard for some of you. Your self-regard may be low. You may have a family history that is not conducive to acceptance. But this step is vital to creating great relationships. We all are human beings. We all have limitations. Some of us try to cover those limitations in a variety of ways. Others wallow in them. If you have completed step one, you know your strengths and weaknesses. Of course, you can work on your weaknesses and try to improve them. That is probably a good thing. But you can accept yourself with all of your limitations, especially those you cannot change. Don't worry so much about your physical appearance or other things that bother you about yourself. If they bother you, that will translate to others.

I'll give you a very practical example: Have you ever tried desperately to get someone to like you, and they wouldn't give you the time of day? Then when you started a relationship with someone else, what happened? Usually the people you were pursuing come out of the woodwork and want to be with you. Why do you think that is? Did all of them change? It is more likely that because you are in a relationship, you feel better about yourself and create a different emotional energy. People are drawn to that energy and want to be around you. This will take some effort, but you can develop a love for yourself. If that's too hard, try just accepting yourself. Once you start accepting yourself for who you are with all of your limitations, you will draw people to you. And it will be easier to accept others.

Step 3: Expand your knowledge

Learn as much as you can about as many different subjects as you can, even the ones that don't interest you. Know a little bit about a lot of different things. Many technical folks have knowledge that is an inch wide and a mile deep. Try to develop knowledge that is an inch deep and a mile wide. I've found that the people who can develop relationships quickly have a lot of different interests. You don't have to become an expert. You just have to have a thirst for knowledge. Turn off the television and read more. If you can read a book a week, you will increase your knowledge dramatically. Most of the people you look up to are likely readers and searchers for knowledge. Learn more. Keep up with current events as best you can. Know how things work. Become a trivia hound. Know about other cultures. Travel more. Develop a sense of wonder about the world. The more you know, the more you will be able to relate to others.

I'm not a NASCAR fan, but I know enough about it to carry on a decent conversation with others about it. And many of my clients are NASCAR fans. They love talking about it. I ask them who their favorite driver is and why. I ask them about the current standings and their favorite tracks. I ask them why someone from California should be allowed to be a driver in NASCAR. My brother, Ben, is a master at this. With his knowledge of so many different things, he would be comfortable talking to just about anyone.

And even if you know nothing about a subject, you can still make this work. Admit to the other person that you know nothing about the subject and ask them to tell you about it. If it is something that they are passionate about, they will certainly fill you in.

One caveat here: Don't become a bore with your knowledge. Don't be like Cliff Claven from the old Cheers television show. Use your knowledge to make connections, not to show how smart you are.

Step 4: Try to get perspectives on different values and cultures

This also goes for gender differences. Learn about and appreciate the differences while emphasizing the similarities. When it comes down to it, we are all human beings who have a need to love and be loved. Find that common connection. For some difficult people your only connection may be that you are both carbon-based life forms. If you can travel more, this is like getting a PhD in relationships. Find out about different cultures, food, art, music, dance, and language. Learn a language if you can. Learn about cultural differences with greetings, meetings, social situations, and business situations. There are thousands of books on cultural differences.

Also, learn about gender differences and how men and women approach things differently. I recently went on a yoga retreat that was organized by Helen, a friend of mine. To my shock and pleasant surprise, out of 35 participants, I was the only male.

This was a big learning experience for me. The first night, everyone met for dinner. Keep in mind that no one knew each other. Now I had been to these first night dinners with groups of men. The first night with a group of men, you will see the following: All of the men will talk about their position at work, what they do, and what monumental projects or concerns they've been involved with. They tend to boast about their successes and retell stories of how they overcame difficulties. They have all been on the worst project ever built. There is a hierarchy established from the outset. There is a pecking order. Men connect with manly hobbies like sports, hunting, fishing, and motorcycles.

The experience with the group of women was completely different. The first question out of every woman's mouth was, "How do you know Helen?" They wanted to how I came to be there. They wanted to know how I fit in with everyone else. What was my connection with Helen? Immediately they tried to establish those connections and networks. Connections and group harmony are paramount to many groups of women. Most of the time, there are no hierarchies established. Everyone is made to participate and feel as if they are part of the group. I think this goes back to childhood. Little boys play games like king of the hill and follow the leader. Little girls play more collaborative games. And if there is a girl who wants to take over and be the leader, she is shunned from the group for being "too bossy".

It doesn't matter of you are a man or a woman. Take note. When you know about these dynamics and make an effort to understand these differences, you will be able to create connections with anyone in any situation and establish great relationships.

Step 5: Be open, genuine, and positive

It is a choice. Smile often. It puts people at ease. Humor not only puts people at ease, it actually cements human relationships. Okay tough guys, I know. Smile often? What is he trying to do to us? Don't worry. Your face won't crack. I promise. Being open and genuine and positive is important, especially during those first few seconds. If you approach someone and you are closed off, unsmiling or negative, they will likely not hang around very long. Even a neutral face can be interpreted as someone who is closed off. And remember, being positive is a choice.

What is your dominant style? Is it negative? Neutral? If it is not open, genuine and positive, think hard about turning that around. People like to be around positive people. And that optimism and energy can be cultivated and developed. We teach optimism to people every day. It can be learned and improved. But it starts with a choice. Try reading any of the books by Martin Seligman. He is an expert in positive psychology.

Step 6: Develop a deep and genuine love or at least acceptance of other people

Accept others with all of their limitations. This can be difficult. But once you accept yourself, it's much easier. I know there are a lot of difficult people out there. There are people you probably consider to be stupid, arrogant, contrary, negative, or full of angst. It's those people that need acceptance the most. Give them that grace. Give them the benefit of the doubt. Expect the best from them. You will be greatly amazed at how your attitude will affect theirs.

When you come across these difficult people, think of them as your teacher. They will teach you how to establish great relationships with any person in any situation. Also, their annoying behavior becomes less annoying. There is a great method for bridging those difficult gaps. It was developed by a man named Marshall Rosenberg and it is called Nonviolent Communication. There are four steps:

a. Observe without judgment. Be objective and evaluate the situation.

b. Notice your feelings. Check in with yourself.

c. Identify needs, both yours and theirs. What are you both trying to attain?

d. Make a request. Tell them what you want, taking into account their needs as well.

This is a simple and powerful way to diffuse difficult situations, but it takes practice. Try it!

When I was a project manager, we had a project with a particularly difficult owner's representative. I was having a beer with a few other project managers who had the same owner's representative on past projects. They told me that this person was a real jerk, unreasonable, and downright mean. I conveyed to them that I got along great with him and that he was quite reasonable. They thought I was lying. But it was true. I didn't know all of these negative things being said about him, so I treated him nicely. I grew the relationship and the project was easy and fun. My approach to him allowed him to act differently.

Step 7: The first five seconds

What are you supposed to do during the introduction? How should you act? Is it really that important? According to numerous studies, that first impression is vital. In the first few seconds, people will judge your intelligence, your socio-economic status, if you are a good person or not, whether or not they like you, and if you are successful or not. We utilize a process in our brain known as the adaptive unconscious. It allows us to do something called thin slicing. Malcolm Gladwell talks about this in his book, *Blink*. A study was done with a college professor. They asked students to rate his teaching ability after watching three fifteen second videos of him teaching. They rated the professor the same as the students who spent a semester with him. Then, they cut the video clips down to five seconds. The results were the same. The point is, we can determine an awful lot with a minimum amount of information. This is very good for most things. The downside to this ability is stereotyping. First impressions aren't always right. And you can always overcome poor first impressions, but why should you have to?

We do an exercise where I introduce myself several different ways and then ask the group to write down their impressions of me. It's amazing the assumptions they make based on a two second encounter. But they do. They will say that I am arrogant, incompetent, shy, mean, angry, or whatever they perceive for that particular introduction. The last introduction is a normal introduction where I relax, smile, make eye contact and use a nice, firm handshake. So let me ask you. What first impression do you create when you meet someone? And if you don't know the answer to that question, you should definitely find out.

When you are going into a situation where you will be introducing yourself, be deliberate about what you are conveying. Be relaxed, open, smiling, and calm. Make good eye contact and give a nice, firm handshake. Slow your mind down and be prepared to listen for the person's name. It's called "original awareness". You can't remember anything that you are not aware of. Be deliberate in your quest to remember the person's name. Repeat it, write it down, write down a short, physical description, whatever it takes to remember their name.

Many people say that they remember the face, but can't recall the name. So the trick is to associate the face with the name. Whenever I meet someone named John, I think of John the Baptist. I picture their chopped off head on a silver platter with blood and veins below it. When I see them, the name John automatically pops into my head.

You can remember names by making these ridiculous associations. If you know someone with that same name, picture the two people together with a ridiculous visual image. If you want to be really adept at remembering names, get *The Memory Book* by Jerry Lucas. There is an entire chapter devoted to remembering names. I have recently been made aware of a phenomenon that affects a small percentage of the population. It's called face blindness. These people have a cognitive disconnect that doesn't allow them to remember faces, even people they know well.

I was giving an introduction to emotional intelligence to a group of forty geotechnical engineers. They all filed into a large warehouse for a dinner the night before our day of work together. There was also a speaker and two caterers from a local Mexican restaurant. Everyone introduced themselves to me. At the end of the night, I asked them if they wanted a preview for tomorrow. I asked them if they knew everyone there. Since they were from several different offices, they did not. So I introduced all forty people. I also introduced the speaker and the two guys from the Mexican restaurant. They were very impressed, and it created more work for me with their company. Believe me, you can do this. I'm not particularly smart, and I don't have a photographic memory. It's just a little technique and a lot of practice.

At these networking events, people usually give you their business card. Don't be too quick to shove it in your pocket. In Asian cultures, the business card represents the person, so you should never write on it or put it in your pocket. They will give you their business card with both hands usually with a slight bow. They will scrutinize your card and usually make a comment on it. I'm not sure that you have to bow, but I think it makes a great impression to actually read the card and make a comment on it.

During that short encounter, find out as much as you can about that person. Is he married? Does he have kids? What are his hobbies? What school did he go to? Then, write down some of these factoids, and later, put it into your contact database. Also, put down when and where you met him and any other pertinent facts. How many contacts do you have in your database right now that you have no idea who the person is?

Whenever you are in conversation with a person, be fully engaged and mindful of the person who is in front of you. They are the only person in the world as far as you are concerned. Don't look at your watch or your computer screen or your Blackberry. Don't be distracted. Be with them fully. For a coffee or lunch meeting, you may want to say to them that you are turning your phone off so you won't be interrupted. Put your laser beam focus on them. Make them feel important and valued. Make them believe that you are genuinely interested in them and what they have to say. This may be difficult with some people, but even with those difficult people, practice this full engagement. It is important.

Step 8: The second encounter

First of all, you are going to remember their name. They will likely not remember yours, so that gives you an advantage. Introduce yourself so they won't be embarrassed about not remembering your name. Then, talk about them. Let them know that you remember them and those pertinent facts. You may need to refer to your phone and the contact information. That's okay. Then ask some good leading questions and let them talk. Find out even more about them. And when you gather more information, put it into your contact database. You can also put the time and place of this second meeting. Don't ever think that you will remember these details. Just document it.

Find the common threads with this person. With expanded knowledge, you can find common threads with just about anyone. The second encounter is perfect for exploring those things that you might have in common. Again, ask those questions and let them know that you know something about the things that are important to them. You don't have to agree with everything that they value or find important. The main thing is to let them know that you have some kind of connection with them. For some people, this may be difficult, but if you are persistent, you will find something.

Step 9: Make it all about them

The key to creating a great connection with someone is to be interested, not interesting. People aren't really interested in what you are doing or saying, only in what they are doing or saying. This is the cardinal rule of being a good conversationalist. An interesting story I heard some time ago (it may be true or not) is of a lady who had the pleasure of sitting next to two British Prime Ministers at dinners on two successive weeks. The first week was Lord George, and the second was Disraeli.

After the experiences someone asked her to compare the two. Her reply was, "After sitting next to Lord George I concluded that he was the most important person in the world. After sitting next to Disraeli I concluded I was the most important person in the world". Disraeli was intensely interested in her, not in talking about himself. When you observe successful talk show hosts on television, seldom will you find them talking about themselves. Rather, they are filled with questions for the guest of the week. Of course that's their job, but it serves as a convenient showcase to gain the feeling of being with a person who doesn't talk about themselves.

Step 10: Food and Drink

Break bread together or have a beer or cocktail together. Eating and drinking are intimate acts. Continue to talk about mutual interests. Also be prepared to talk about the interests of the other person even if they are not your own. This is a very important step in a relationship. One networker calls these FDOs (Food and Drink Opportunities). Keith Ferrazzi is a master networker. His book, *Never Eat Alone*, talks about being relentless in your pursuit of connections with others. And everyone has to eat and drink. And everyone likes it when you buy them lunch.

Find interesting places to meet. Out of the way restaurants and coffee shops with great atmospheres are very conducive to getting people to relax and open up. Use this often to further develop your relationships.

Step 11: Create networks

Networks are powerful things. You can have formal and informal networks. Most people have the wrong idea about networking. They think it is about introducing yourself, shoving your business card in the other guy's hand and then he calls you and you get his business. WRONG! Bob Littell's book, *Netweaving,* takes a different approach that works quite well. He follows these steps to establish relationships. At networking events, his approach is to find out as much about the other person and their business as possible and ask them if there is anything you can do to help their business.

Don't sell people on yourself or your company. This is a real turnoff and a big mistake. Your encounters will avoid you like a plague. Again, make it all about them and let them know that you are there to help them and their business. Ask them what they are struggling with. Also, with your wide network of people you are amassing a great deal of expertise and knowledge. Try to find people that you can introduce to each other. Perhaps it's a common personal or professional interest. Or perhaps one person has a solution that the other person needs. Either way, when you solve their problem for them, they are going to remember you and recommend you to others.

Have you tried any of the online social networks? They can be a powerful way to build a large network in a very short period of time. I'm signed up on several of them. There are ones for business like Plaxo and Linked In and there are others that are more geared toward the personal like Twitter and Facebook.

a. This first step is very simple. Visit these websites and create a profile. If it is strictly for business and not personal, be sure to pack your profile with your accomplishments and qualifications. If it is personal, you can also add some personal information. By the way, personal information can be very beneficial in the business profiles as well. You can tell a lot about a person by where they focus their time and energy. Be sure to add a good photo. Make your profile attractive and full of good information about you and your business.

b. Start creating connections with people. Most of these sites have a feature where it will scan your Outlook or other contact database and find everyone on their network that is in your address book. Or you can do your own searches for individuals and ask them to create a connection with you. However you do this, you must start trolling for people. Find the ones you want to connect with and ask them to connect with you. Delve into all the companies you used to work for. Explore all of the groups you have had contact with in the past.

It's easy to find people now thanks to Google. I found an old boss of mine by Googling his name and the word "construction", and I had not had any contact with him for over 20 years. I found him working for a contractor in Houston, Texas. It was not only great to catch up and see what he has been up to, but this was a great business contact for me. He wanted to read my book, which may lead to future work for my company.

I try to make connections all the time with email and phone calls. Most of the time, there is no response. Despite numerous attempts, they would not return my phone calls or emails. But when I sent out an invitation via Linked In, they accepted it quickly, usually within a few minutes. Somehow, these sites lend legitimacy to that outreach.

c. Once you have a list of people whom you want to stay connected with, all you have to do is occasionally write a few lines about what you are doing. You may pose a question. You may post a photo or video or link to some interesting websites, videos, or articles. You can write as much or as little as you want except for Twitter, where you are limited to 140 characters.

d. You may want to program these sites to send the notifications to your mobile phone. This is very easy to do. You can always block this later if it gets to be too much.

e. You may recommend people and ask them to recommend you. This is very easy to do. There are usually links to do that on the website. Build up your reviews in order to create credibility.

f. You may join groups or start groups. This can be helpful for networking, for best practices, for idea exchanges, support, or encouragement. Try to find as many groups as practical. There are many possibilities for groups: alumni groups, industry groups, special interest groups, high schools, colleges, preconstruction folks, cancer survivors, church groups, study groups, or hobbies.

g. You may use these networks internally to stay in touch with a select group of people, perhaps a project team or an internal preconstruction group. When someone posts a comment, it can be automatically sent to everyone. It's quicker than email and can be a great way to exchange information and receive feedback. It's the Nextel of the web.

h. If you are attending a conference, you can find groups of people either geographically or an industry group that you can contact and let them know that you will be in attendance. Ask them if they would like to meet for a cup of coffee, a drink, lunch, or dinner. Use every opportunity to connect with all of the people in your contacts.

i.   Try to check your social networks as often as possible. Keep your profile updated. Send out blasts to people and look for new connections. Find some interesting things to post that will intrigue people and compel them to stay in touch with you. This is a big key. You must check these at least once per week. If people are reaching out to you and you don't reach back, they will likely drop you.

Step 12: Follow up, follow up, follow up

Now that you have all of this vital information in your contact database, use it. Send out cards for birthdays and anniversaries. Send out thank you notes. Although much of this can be done electronically, I prefer to send handwritten notes. People receive so few handwritten notes these days, that they will likely read it and respond in a positive way. People are so overwhelmed by email, your message may be sent to spam or deleted without being read.

Send notes congratulating your contact on a new project, a new job, a big win for their college team, or an award. Send them links to cool websites or articles. Again, this contact should not be self-promoting. Make it all about them and send them things that they would be interested in reading or seeing.

I met an engineer at a design company. We talked briefly and he mentioned to me that his wife was the CEO of Children's Healthcare in Atlanta. He gave me his card, and I put him in my database. I remembered what he told me. A week later, there was an article in the paper saying that Children's Healthcare was named one of the top pediatric hospitals in the country. I sent him an email giving him a link to the article and said that he must be very proud of his wife. I have done a lot of work for this company.

Part 2
Common Courtesy

Common Courtesy

"Courtesy opens many doors." Fortune Cookie

For most tough guys, courtesy is seen as weakness. But I can tell you that courtesy does, indeed, open many doors. If you utilize your courtesy skills, you can be comfortable in any situation, and people will want to be around you. They will want to work for you. It will ensure your success. Because courtesy succeeds even with people who are not courteous. And in these tough fields like construction, there are many discourteous people that you must deal with.

What has happened to common courtesy? It is much like common sense. It's not so common these days. In a phone survey of 2,013 adults taken by a group called Public Agenda in January of 2003, "a lack of respect and courtesy in American society is a serious problem." Sixty-one percent of the people surveyed believe it has become worse in recent years.

I was raised in the South where we were brought up to be Southern gentlemen. We were taught to say "sir" and 'ma'm'. We were taught to respect our elders, to give up our seats to women and older folks, to open doors, to pick up the check, and to share whatever we had. In short, our momma tried to raise us right.

But our wonderfully diverse society now seems to have a problem with these simple examples of common courtesy. This problem may stem from our increased social isolation manifesting itself in the form of too much television, video games, movies, and the internet. This causes a lack of direct social interaction and is especially true of the younger generations. The lack of basic human support systems such as the family unit and local community organizations add to this problem. Another reason may be the abundance of so many cultures with very different values. But whatever the reasons, we need to take a look at these issues and make a concerted effort to re-establish common courtesy in our society. It is not only a nice thing to do, but I believe the future of our society and of our world may depend on this very simple thing.

I notice that whenever I give in to bad attitudes and rude people, whenever I become angry and rude, the situation always takes a downward spiral. But as an experiment, I tried to be nice in these situations. I tried to be overly nice. I tried to turn the other cheek. And most of the time, whenever I was nice and courteous, the outcome was markedly different. Most situations ended positively.

A younger man asked an old man the secret to his long marriage. The old man replied, "Well, son, let me tell you. You can be right, or you can be happy." That is true for most of the difficult situations we encounter. Don't try to be right. You don't need to be right. All you need to do is try to make things work out in a positive way.

This is not just about getting what you want. It's also about karma. I know, tough guy, you think karma is something for the soft and weak. But think about it. In the weeks following September 11th, everyone was genuinely nice to each other, not just in the US, but all over the world. I was in Prague during the 9/11 attacks. After the attacks, the airports were shut down. We could not get home even if we wanted to. The hotel where I was staying offered to house all Americans for free until they could return home. Every restaurant I went into would not let me pay for my meal when they heard my US accent. There was an outpouring of humanity and common courtesy. They were being nice to me, and it made a tremendous difference.

Imagine for a moment if we could sustain that level of courtesy. We would be so busy being nice, that many of our global ideological conflicts would be put into perspective. Courtesy would transcend culture, religion, and language. Our work would become more joyful. Our relationships would be more satisfying. Then, we could begin to build bridges of understanding throughout the world.

 The Tools

Use the Magic Words

As a small child, I watched the Captain Kangaroo show every day. On that show, the magic words were "please" and "thank you". You could get almost anything you wanted by using these words. On the other hand, if you didn't use those words, you never received what you asked for. It was like magic. It may sound too simple to be true, but this is the foundation for courtesy. Use these words often and with sincerity, and you will be surprised how the magic will begin to work. One other very important magic word is "sorry". You can diffuse many volatile situations by saying "I'm sorry". You can also say "bless you" when someone sneezes. Variations of this phrase are used in many cultures after a sneeze. In Southern Europe and parts of South America, they say "salut", in Sweden, "prosit".

Whenever someone does something nice, write them a thank you note. If possible, make this a handwritten note. People receive a lot of emails, and your e-card may get lost in the shuffle. But people very rarely receive snail mail anymore. They will open and read your note. My wife is the queen of thank you notes and writes them often. This is a tangible "thank you" and is always appreciated.

Be Sincere

You can't just *use* the magic words. You have to mean them. My wife encountered a situation with an airline where the company did not deliver what they promised. In each piece of correspondence, they apologized profusely and vowed to correct the situation. The only problem was that they never corrected anything. The apologies became a source of frustration instead of a bridge to understanding. So be sincere and follow through. Some folks in the programs think that keeping track of personal details in your phone and computer is somehow insincere. Keith Ferrazzi, the master of creating relationships says, "Just because it's intentional doesn't mean it's insincere."

Use the Platinum Rule

We all know the Golden Rule. Do unto others as you would have them do unto you. But do you know the Platinum Rule? Treat others the way they want to be treated, which, in some cases, may be different than the way you want to be treated. Of course, there are times that we don't always practice either of these rules. There are predictable times when we forget it. By keeping the Platinum Rule in the back of your head, you will be surprised at how effective you can handle most situations. Take a moment and ask yourself, "If I were sitting behind that counter or in that toll booth, or across from me at this table, how would I want to be treated?"

Use Empathy, walk around in their moccasins for a while

Plato said, "Be kind, for everyone you meet is fighting a hard battle." Always try to put yourself into the shoes of the person with whom you are dealing. The next time you are in a fast food line or returning an item, try to take into account the person behind that counter. They are in a low-paying, fast-paced, high stress job, and they often encounter frustrated, angry, rude people. Perhaps they are in a poor economic situation, lack higher education, or are immigrants who speak very little English.

Would it improve the situation if you asked them how their day was going? Or told them that you thought they had a difficult job and appreciated their efforts? You may also talk about some skill they possess that you admire. I am always impressed by skilled receptionists who can greet visitors and answer dozens of phone calls at the same time. If I had to be a receptionist, I know I would be a terrible one. I simply don't possess those skills. Let people know that you appreciate them for the skills they possess. If you establish this connection with them, you will be more likely to receive excellent service.

Service employees should remember that customers may be angry and upset. If you simply smile, use a clear voice, see their point of view and use "please", "thank you" and "I'm sorry", it is often possible to disarm their anger.

As Emily Post, the guru of etiquette, said, "Manners are a sensitive awareness of the feelings of others. If you have that awareness, you have good manners, no matter what fork you use."

Speak Clearly

One thing that destroys personal encounters faster than anything is basic communication. Many times, people don't speak clearly, distinctly, or with the proper volume. This problem may be cultural, it may be a personality trait or it may be a problem with the language.

If you speak slowly, distinctly, and loudly enough to be heard, many of your encounters will go more smoothly. In addition, since communication is up to 95% non-verbal, overt sign language may help. I was in a Big Lots recently, and a young woman was asking for a product. She spoke to one of the Big Lots representatives, who was Russian. The woman asked if they had a "stawa". That is exactly what I heard from her mouth, "stawa".

In addition to that pronunciation, she said it in a very soft voice. The Big Lots representative did not understand and asked her to repeat it several times. Finally, the exasperated woman stormed out. The Russian woman was at a loss. I finally figured out that the young woman was saying "stop watch". If she had spoken slowly, distinctly, with the right amount of volume, or if she had mimed using a stopwatch, the Russian woman probably would have understood what she wanted.

A similar thing happened at a local jewelry store. An older man wanted to "get a clas put on this hyere braylet". There were several stares from the woman behind the counter, who was from Cuba. The man decided that she didn't speak English well and asked to speak to someone else. Another woman came from the back, who was from India. The man rolled his eyes and looked exasperated. Now he had to speak to another "foreigner" who also would not understand him. He asked her if the jeweler could "put a clas on the braylet". I finally understood and told the Indian woman that he wanted a clasp put on his bracelet. The man seemed relieved to have a translator available to make his wishes known.

You can see from these examples how important it is to simply be heard. So, speak slowly, distinctly, and with proper volume. Do your best to communicate well. It will go a long way. If English is a second language or you have a strong regional dialect, this is even more important. In these cases try to speak as clearly as you can. And if you are listening, listen carefully and ask people to repeat if necessary.

If you encounter someone who doesn't speak clearly, tell them that you are hard of hearing and ask them to speak up and speak slowly. This will put all the blame on you, but it will get them to communicate better, and it's more courteous than saying, "I can't understand you." or "Why don't you learn to speak English?" or "Would you quit mumbling?".

Call them by their name

If they have name tags, call them by their name. When people hear their name, they are pleasantly surprised. As Dale Carnegie says, everyone likes to hear their own name. This can put a person at ease instantly. Of course, you don't want to overdo this and come across like a bad salesman.

Smile!

I know, tough guy. Your face may crack. But give it a try. The world is not such a serious place. This is the number one thing I have to keep reminding my participants, to smile more. A smile transcends all languages and cultures. Even if you are feeling tired, frustrated, or impatient, you can smile and put the other person at ease. This will make your encounter more pleasant no matter what the circumstances. This is especially true when you speak over the phone. People can hear the smile in your voice.

Use humor if you can

Humor can diffuse tough situations and give you perspective on things. Here are a few examples:

I was returning a close-out item to an office supply store. The store policy was that close-outs could not be returned. But this particular item was missing a part that was essential to its operation. I repeatedly explained this to the woman behind the counter, and she repeated that it was their policy that they could not accept this as a return. I explained myself several times, and she quoted the policy several times. Finally she asked, "Are you an idiot?" I answered in a very polite and non-sarcastic way, "Why yes, as a matter of fact, I am an idiot. I come from a long line of idiots. My father was an idiot and his father before him. And before we came to this country, my great-great-grandfather was the village idiot. It's sort of a family tradition." She actually laughed and the tension was gone. She apologized and told me that she had not slept the night before and had a very rough day. She gave me a store credit despite the "company policy".

I was on the phone with a bank. They were trying very hard to understand, but the point was not getting across, and we were both getting a bit frustrated with the situation. They didn't seem to understand that I had two American Express Accounts. They had electronically paid one on time, but the other one was late and I was assessed a finance charge. Finally I said, "Thanks for being patient with me. I'm sure I have some responsibility in this situation. Perhaps I put the electronic payment request in too late." This softened them up a bit, and they said that perhaps they had some responsibility in the matter. Then, I said to them, "Wait a minute. I'm a little confused about one thing. Aren't you a big bank? Aren't you supposed to tell me that it is all my fault and transfer me to ten different people?" We all had a good laugh, the tension was gone, and we resolved the situation. They ended up paying the finance charge for me.

Children and Pets

If you have children and/or dogs, cats, birds, gerbils, or fish, please keep one thing in mind: nobody loves them as much as you do. You may not mind that your pets jump on you or lick your face or put their nose up your crotch. But other people do mind. You may not mind your children being loud or jumping on you or covering your head with whipped cream. Be aware that your friends, neighbors, and relatives may mind these things. Keep your children and pets well-behaved.

If someone needs help, offer to help them

If you see someone broken down on the highway, looking lost or having a problem with a copier, a vending machine, or ATM, offer to help if you think you can do so safely. There are exceptions, of course. If you are alone and see a man with a bloody hockey mask and a chain saw on the side of the road, you should probably keep driving. When you do stop and help someone, try to do this without any expectations of payment or being thanked. This spreads good karma. Sometimes the person needing help will offer to pay you for your trouble. If they do this, you may want to tell them that they should do something nice for someone else and use the "pay it forward" concept.

One time, I helped an elderly couple change a tire on the interstate highway. They had been waiting for someone to help them for four hours, and they told me I was their guardian angel. When they offered to pay me, I said, "We don't use money in heaven".

Try to be diplomatic, especially if the person has a disability. Try to avoid the word "need". Instead of saying, "Do you need help?", try saying, "May I help you with that?" You should not help the person without asking. It allows them the option to accept your help.

If you see someone struggling to open a door, simply open it for them. It's nice to open a door for someone even if they don't "need" it. They usually appreciate it. When you go through a door, look back and see if you can hold the door for the next person.

Be on time

We are all busy. Most of us are extremely busy. But we should not use that as an excuse for being late. Sometimes there are circumstances beyond our control, but those are very rare. If you plan for those things that can go wrong, you will rarely be late. To be late shows disrespect for the other person's time and begins any encounter on a bad note. So be on time, start meetings on time, and pick people up on time. And if you do have to be late, call them, let them know you are going to be late, tell them you are sorry, ask them to please forgive you, and thank them for being so understanding.

If you don't start a meeting on time, you will actually encourage people to be late for the next meeting.

Furthermore, it penalizes those who are on time. One time my wife asked a subordinate why he always came late to meetings. He replied that there were several others who were always late, so he didn't want to arrive too early. With this attitude a downward spiral occurs. The people arrive late, then the meeting starts later, then the people start arriving later, then the meeting starts even later, and so on and so on.

When running a management development program for a multi-national construction company, we had a rule if the participants were late. They had to sing a song in front of the entire group at dinner that evening. This seemed to work fairly well except for this one Danish guy who loved to sing. He intentionally came in late so that he could sing in the evenings. So form your rules carefully.

There are exceptions to this. When I did a program in Argentina, I found that everyone was consistently fifteen to thirty minutes "late". Being on time is not part of their culture and you have to be aware of those differences.

Turn off your mobile device!

In public places, try to be aware of other people and put your mobile telephone on vibrate. That loud ringing is annoying and distracting, especially in public places such as movies, libraries, parks, and restaurants.

Our phones now beep and chirp when email arrives. Turn them off or put them on vibrate. This can also be a time management issue. If you turn these devices off for periods of time and check them in batches, you can make more efficient use of your time.

If you ever have a one-on-one meeting with someone such as a business meeting or lunch, it is good courtesy to turn your mobile phone off during these times. There are rare exceptions, of course such as a pregnant wife or an illness in the family that requires monitoring. If you have an exception, tell the person beforehand that you may have to answer your phone. But these circumstances are very rare. I don't know many people or circumstances that have that level of importance.

For the development program I mentioned before, we also had the champagne rule. If anyone's mobile phone rang during a session, that participant had to buy a round of drinks for everyone in the group. And since the group had as many as 30 people, absent-mindedness became quite expensive. One time a phone was on vibrate, vibrated across the table and fell on the floor. Even though it didn't ring, it distracted the group, and we charged that participant with the champagne penalty.

Don't be in a rush if you can help it

If you're rushing around, pressed for time and think that you are going to zip in and out to renew your license or return that piece of merchandise, then you are setting yourself up to fail. You are putting yourself in a situation that will most likely have a poor outcome. If you don't have the time for potentially time consuming tasks, then try to put them off to a later time. Plan ahead so that you are not rushed as the deadline approaches. When you are not rushed, you will be able to relax and think about the concepts in this book.

Be aware of cultural differences

There are many different cultures in the USA, and most have different values. Some cultures seem more tolerant of things like waiting or profanity. Some of these values are drawn along socio-economic lines. Remember this and try to act accordingly. In many cases, the people you are dealing with are not attempting to annoy. They may be acting as their culture or socio-economic background dictates. In these cases, you must be more diligent with your courtesy. Many times, when we become angry at these people, and they happen to be from a different culture, we resort to stereotyping. Imagine if we could get beyond that stereotyping and make a true connection with these people. What a difference that would make.

Cultural differences don't only happen with people from other countries. We have definite cultural differences right here in the USA. The South has a different pace and different rules than the North. In the Public Agenda survey, it was found that there was a big split on the use of profanity from North to South. Three out of four Southerners said it is always wrong to take God's name in vain, while half of those surveyed from the Northeast said that there is nothing wrong with it or it falls in the gray area. There is also an East coast, West coast split. Just because people live their lives at a different pace and have different beliefs, tolerances, prejudices, and priorities, doesn't mean you can't make a connection with them. Find the common thread and use it to build a relationship.

Be aware of things like eye contact, personal space requirements, and physical contact because they vary from culture to culture. These cultural differences are usually discussed in travel books. Please pay attention to them and respect them. Asian cultures have different personal space requirements and rarely look you in the eye for any period of time. Americans like that strong handshake, but this can be misconstrued in some cultures as an act of aggression.

If you can learn a little about other people's culture and learn a few key phrases in their language, you can deal with any situation much more effectively.

 The Situations

Returns/Checkouts/Restaurants/Fast Food/Retail

In the Public Agenda survey, nearly half of those surveyed had walked out of a store in the past year because of "poor customer service". When dealing with service personnel, try to remain patient and calm while in line. You may want to bring a book, an audio book, or some music to pass the time in case there are delays. Personally, I take this type of opportunity to go over some positive affirmations.

Smile when it is your turn and ask how the person is doing today. Calmly explain what you would like. Remember, this person may encounter angry, impatient people all day long. Fill the conversation with "please" and "thank you" and call the person by name. Never demand. Use phrases like "I'm sorry to bother you" or "Can you do me a favor?" This usually gets better results than being demanding.

If they make a mistake, don't be too quick to point it out. Instead of saying, "Hey, I ordered this with no pickle!", perhaps you could say something along the lines of "I'm sorry, I may be wrong, I probably am, but I thought I ordered this without pickles. Would it be too much trouble to make me another sandwich?" You can usually gain a lot by saying "It's probably my fault" even if it isn't. But to place blame sets up a confrontation and resistance. While this may appear self-deprecating, it usually gets results.

When checking out at the grocery store, please don't get in the express lane unless you have the right number of items. If you see someone with only a few items, let them go ahead of you. Think how pleased you are when someone does that for you. When you aren't in a rush, you can afford this courtesy.

Being pulled over

When you are pulled over, the first thing to do is relax. If you have done something wrong, you are likely to get a ticket. Remember, police officers put their lives on the line for you every day. Imagine that you are a police officer and you are paid very little to do a difficult job. The last thing you want is a citizen who is angry at you because they broke the law. If you didn't break the law, you will always have the opportunity to explain it in court. Don't take it out on the officer. You can talk to them about how difficult their job is and how they don't get paid enough. A good thing to do is apologize for breaking the law. Don't offer excuses. It doesn't help. Smile and be nice. You would be surprised at the number of tickets that are dismissed.

I had this happen to me recently. I was pulled over for speeding in another neighborhood. We are always trying to get people to slow down in our neighborhood, but there

I was doing 50 in a 25. I told the officer that I appreciated everything that he did for us, and that I was glad he pulled me over. I told him that I had become one of those people that I dislike, speeding through a residential area. He was quite shocked. He still gave me ticket, but reduced the speed I was traveling and told me how to plead *nolo contendre* so that it would not show up on my driving record. After that, I made a conscious effort to slow down and drive the speed limit, especially in residential areas.

Work situations

First of all, be on time for all meetings. For breaks and lunches, use only the allotted time and no more. Just because you are being paid doesn't mean that you don't have to be nice. People respond to nice. Say please and thank you, especially to subordinates. Write thank you notes. This is a tangible way of using the magic words "thank you", and it is always appreciated. On one project, I wrote a thank you note to all of the mechanical, electrical, and plumbing superintendents. The plumbing superintendent told me that in 20 years, he had never received a thank you note. He took it home and showed his family. His wife put it on the refrigerator next to their kids' artwork. Whenever I needed anything, this superintendent was there for me. I have also given massage certificates to subordinates for a job well done. These kinds of tangible thank yous create loyalty and increase performance.

Well placed humor is also appreciated in the work place. A subordinate came to me upset about the way a certain project was progressing. The deadline loomed nearer and nearer, and she was hitting brick walls at every turn. In addition, her personal life was difficult as she was going through a divorce. She was nearly in tears when she came to me, overwhelmed by everything. I told her not to worry. I was going to help her. She looked relieved. Then I said, "The first thing we must do is . . . go and get a cup of coffee." She looked at me incredulously and laughed. "Are you serious?" she asked. "Yes", I replied, and we went to a local coffee shop.

By getting away from the office and relaxing a bit, she was able to get some perspective on the problem. When we returned to the office, she tackled her project with renewed vigor and completed it on time. All she needed was to break the tension and loosen up a bit.

The Platinum Rule should always be in effect at work. Be aware of how co-workers feel and talk to them about things that are important to them whether it is work-related or not. I had to motivate a project team to do something, but could not get through to the project leader. One day, I found out that he liked bowling and was on tour as a professional bowler at one time. From then on, I started all conversations with how is your game? After that, the project proceeded smoothly.

Being a good audience member

When you go to a concert or theater or movie, there are some things you should keep in mind. If you are late, sit in the back. Don't go down front and walk over people who are trying to enjoy the event. If you are a tall person, have big hair or wear a hat, be mindful of where you sit, especially if you are in a theater that does not have stadium seating. Don't block other's line of sight. Turn off your mobile device. Don't talk during the performance. If you are one of those people who go to the restroom or to buy refreshments during the show or performance, sit on the aisle and in the back. Don't bring young children to the show unless it is something like Sponge Bob on ice. They can be annoying to others in the audience.

One of the greatest stories of audience courtesy I have ever heard was a told by Leonard Slatkin, the famous conductor. The orchestra was in Japan. One of the patrons started to cough. When he knew he couldn't control his cough, he covered his mouth, crouched down and ran up the aisle and out of the auditorium so as not to disturb the other patrons. Mr. Slatkin said that in the USA, when the concert is over, several dozen people exit the auditorium quickly without clapping in order to beat the traffic. In Japan, not only did the entire audience clap for the orchestra, but they waited until all of the musicians had left the stage before leaving the auditorium. They did this to show respect and courtesy.

Email

Email is no different than any other form of communication. Be nice. Use please and thank you. Don't write in CAPITAL LETTERS or **BOLD LETTERS** because it means you are **SHOUTING AT THE PERSON!** If appropriate, write on your email that there is no need to send a reply or thank you. Don't forward emails to long lists of people. If you want to forward something to an individual because you think they might enjoy it, that is courteous, but don't overdo it.

If you want to put the best face on your email and increase the chances of someone actually reading it, try the following:

1. Put something interesting in the subject line. If possible, put your entire message in the subject line.

2. If you cannot put the entire message in the subject line, make the email short enough so they can read the entire email without scrolling down.

3. Don't add attachments unless absolutely necessary or if an attachment is expected.

People will appreciate this cyber courtesy. In addition, there is a greater probability that your emails will actually be read.

Let me share with you an email I received from a company where I purchased something online:

We're just checking in to see if you received your order from Better World Books. If your order hasn't blessed your mailbox just yet, heads are gonna roll in the Mishawaka warehouse! Seriously though, if you haven't received your order or are less than 108.8% satisfied, please reply to this message. Let us know what we can do to flabbergast you with service. Thanks again for your support! Humbly Yours, Indaba (our super-cool email robot)

Now that is a cool email that is read and appreciated.

A sign won't do it

We've all seen the signs: DON'T HANG TOWELS OVER THE BALCONY, NO SWIMMING AFTER 10 O'CLOCK, LOADING AND UNLOADING ONLY, EXPRESS LANE-MAXIMUM 12 ITEMS, PLEASE WASH YOUR COFFEE CUP AFTER EACH USE. The problem with signs is that they just don't work very well. Don't think you will fix a problem by installing a sign. In general, people ignore signs. Part of the problem is our independent nature here in the USA. We tend to think that the rules are for all of those other people. There are also problems with literacy and English as a second language. In some large cities, over 200 languages are spoken. Even if you have a sign in Spanish and English, people still may be unable or unwilling to read your well thought out, well-intentioned, problem solving sign. If you want a problem resolved, the best way to do it is face-to-face.

Phone orders/solicitations/phone courtesy

Phone conversations create definite impressions and we should pay more attention to them. Call five businesses from the phone book and see if you can understand the name of the business. From personal experience, most of the time, the name of the business cannot be understood. We tend to mumble, hold the receiver away from our mouths, talk too, fast, and not really listen.

Use your communication skills when you are on the phone. Talk slowly and distinctly. Make sure you truly listen when you encounter voicemail. The message may give you all of the information you need. When leaving a message, always leave your number even if you know they have it. Say it slowly and say it twice so that the other person doesn't have to look up your number to call you back. They may be checking their messages remotely and not have your number with them. If you don't need for them to call you back, say that on the message. It is frustrating to play "phone tag" when a clear, concise message could convey all of the necessary information. You may also want to leave some windows of time to return the call. By making this window clear, you may get more returned calls. Return your messages promptly.

Try to make your outgoing message an interesting one. The same old "sorry we can't be here to take your call . . . " message is boring and lifeless. Be creative. A sample message from my business line (it changes often) is "I can't take your call right now because I am out saving civilization as we know it by training new leaders." If your message is varied and interesting, people are more likely to listen and leave a message. How many times do you hear the answering machine kick in and the caller hangs up before the outgoing message has been completed?

Be especially nice and courteous over the phone because you are only communicating through your voice. Tone, quality, and articulation are essential. Smile when you talk on the phone. The person on the other end will be able to hear when your smile. One company I called answered, "Having a great day at . . . ." What a wonderful way to answer the phone. Also, when I asked for someone there, the receptionist said, "It's my pleasure to connect you." This can be shortened to "my pleasure" if time is an issue.

When receiving calls from telephone solicitors, please try not to get angry. There is no need to ruin your evening or theirs. Simply tell them "sorry, but I'm not interested" and hang up. Another approach is to tell them you are not interested and ask them to remove you from the call list. This isn't the best job in the world, and they probably encounter all kinds of personal attacks before they actually make a sale. In the past, I used an idea from an episode of Seinfeld. I asked the solicitor for his home phone number and told him that I would call him later that evening. When he refused to give me his number, I said, "so, you're telling me that you don't like people to call you at home in the evening?" This worked okay most of the time, but one time the solicitor gave me his phone number and asked me to call him at home any time. This made me realize that these people are just trying to make a living. How can we fault them for that?

If you call a wrong number, please don't hang up or mumble something unintelligible. Simply say, "I'm sorry. I have the wrong number." Then, hang up. If it is very late or very early, apologize for disturbing them.

Dealing with Annoying People

Sometimes we encounter rude and annoying people; that surly server or retail sales person, the guy talking in the movie, the person who cuts in line. How do we deal with these people? Sometimes we ignore them and sometimes we get angry at them. Sometimes we say something and sometimes we let it go. What if we overwhelmed them with nice? Most of the time, being nice works. What if the next time you encountered a surly server you said, "Are you having a bad day? I'm sorry if you're having a bad day."

For the line cutter, you can start by saying to them, "Excuse me. I'm sorry to bother you. Perhaps you didn't know the line started back there. Because I know you wouldn't cut in front of everyone like that because that wouldn't be fair, now would it?"

For the movie talker or cell phone answerer, you can say, "Excuse me, but I wonder if you wouldn't mind turning off your cell phone or stop talking please? I'm really into this movie and each time I hear you talk or answer your cell phone, it pulls me out of it. Thanks for your consideration."

Remember to consider their situation. Sometimes people aren't being rude. There may be circumstances that you don't realize. That man cutting in line may have a pregnant wife in the car about to deliver a baby.

My wife and I had season tickets to the symphony, and the woman in front of us always left early. This annoyed me and my wife. Before one concert, we were chatting with her, and she told us that her husband was bedridden and this was her only time to go out. She always snuck out early because she didn't want to be away from him for too long. That was a good lesson for both of us.

Dealing with Homeless People, Scammers, Panhandlers

If you are approached by a homeless person, you don't have to be rude. You can say something along the lines of "I'm sorry, but I don't have any money to give you right now." Even if you have money in your pocket, you are not telling a lie. There are some people who are scamming for money. They give you a long story about trying to raise enough money for gas and that their family is waiting in the car. Again, you can be nice, but not give in.

Some panhandlers say they want to work, but really only want you to give them money. When I worked for a contractor, I used to give my business card to the people with "will work for food" signs and tell them to call me if they wanted a job. After handing out dozens of cards, I received a phone call from a guy who was a skilled mason.

I arranged for him to go to work for our masonry division, where he worked for several years.

Driving/Road rage/Handicapped parking

Public Agenda's survey said that six drivers in ten regularly see other people driving aggressively or recklessly. More than one-third admitted to occasional bad driving themselves. These road rage incidents, which seem to be on the rise, are dangerous. If you are stuck in traffic, or someone cuts you off, try to let it go. There may be some one who is desperate to get somewhere for a legitimate reason. If you make a mistake or cut someone off, tell them you are sorry. Shrug your shoulders and hit yourself in the head.

Don't drive in the HOV lane unless you have a passenger. Don't drink and drive. Don't pull past the lane lines or pedestrian lines at intersections. They are there for a reason, so pedestrians can walk and so cars will be able to make the turns more easily. If you are past the line, the turning cars have a difficult time and the pedestrians cannot walk across the street. If you are broken down or in an accident, unless there are laws prohibiting it, remove your car from the road. If you see someone broken down, try to give them plenty of room. Go wide around them, in the left lane if possible. Don't drive while talking on the phone unless you can do it hands free and safely. Let people merge. Let people pull ahead of you. Give people plenty of room. Don't block intersections. If you miss a turn or an exit, don't stop and block everything. Keep moving and turn around. Use your turn signals. Don't drive slowly in the fast lane. Slow down in parking lots.

Try this next time you are at a toll booth. Pay for the person behind you. Tell the attendant to tell the next person that you already paid for them and to have a nice day. You never know where small acts of kindness like that may lead.

As for handicapped parking, don't be too quick to judge someone who is trying to take advantage of those coveted parking spots. I know someone who yelled at a person for parking in the handicapped space because they walked normally when they got out of their car. As it turned out, the woman had Multiple Sclerosis that came in episodes. Sometimes she could walk fine. Other times, she needed a cane or a walker. For those of you who don't know, that wide area between handicapped parking spaces is not a parking space. They are areas set aside so that people with handicapped vans will have the room to open their door and deploy their ramp. Please don't park there.

One final note on the use of the word "handicapped". Most people with disabilities find this word offensive. They prefer the term "disabled" or having "special needs". They do not like the euphemisms that use the words "impaired" or "deficient". Deaf people don't believe that their deafness is a handicap and prefer not to be referred to as disabled. Blind people generally prefer the word "blind". They are not "vision impaired" or "deficient in sight".

Waiting room at doctor/dentist/hair appointment

If you are a reader, try to remember to bring a book to read or listen to an audio book. This may help with your patience. If you have the time, and you are at a particularly good part of the book, tell them to take the next person. Be patient and be on time. Part of the reason for backups at these places is that so many people are not on time. Don't pick a time when you have to be rushed.

I did try one thing with a doctor that worked well. I waited for over two hours past my appointed time. When I received my bill, I deducted my billable rate for two hours from the bill and sent it back to him. I did end up paying for the full price of the visit, but I think the doctor got the message. I never waited more than ½ hour after that.

Tipping

If please, thank you, and sorry are magic words, tipping is definitely a magic act. It is especially useful when it is not expected. One time my luggage was lost, and they had a delivery service bring it to my home. I noticed that the delivery guy did this on the side because he used his own car. Perhaps it was a second job. He probably encountered hostile people most of the time. The airlines misplaced their luggage, but the customers probably took it out on him.

He pulled up to the curb at my house, which sets up on a hill. My trip was a month long business trip, so the suitcase was huge and heavy. I walked down to the curb, he unloaded my suitcase, and I gave him a ten dollar bill. I thanked him for bringing my suitcase to me. I'm sure that with most people, he is eager to drop the suitcase quickly and leave before the yelling begins. But he offered to take the suitcase up to the door and into the house. He thanked me several times and told me to have a nice night.

Another example is when my wife and I went to a restaurant with complimentary valet parking. When we left the restaurant, it was pouring down rain. We saw several people in front of us getting their cars, and not one gave the valet a tip. After all, the sign said "free". The valet was soaked to the skin, but used a towel to keep the car seat dry. To my embarrassment, I found that I didn't have any cash to give him a tip. I told him I would give it to him later, and he gave me that look. The one that said, "Yeah, right, buddy." We drove to an ATM and withdrew some cash. We drove back to the restaurant and gave the valet a ten dollar bill. He gave us a broad smile and said, "You have restored my faith in humanity." And we did that all for only ten dollars.

If you are a host or guest in someone's home

It is not difficult to be a good host. Make sure your guests are comfortable. They should have nice place to sleep complete with a few extra pillows and an extra blanket. A reading light is a nice touch as well. Make sure your guests have plenty of towels, wash cloths, toilet paper, shampoo, and other essentials. We keep a basket of soaps and shampoos from hotels for our guests. It is also nice to have some room in the closet for hanging clothes as well as one of those small stands to set a suitcase upon. Let them know that they are welcome and to "make themselves at home".

If you are a guest, you should always leave things better than when you arrived at your host's home. Make your bed. Do your laundry. Do their laundry. Buy groceries and cook a meal. Clean the house or pay to have it cleaned. Be courteous with watching television or listening to music. Always ask if it is okay. Don't monopolize the time with these entertainment centers. Don't use all the hot water. If you have special dietary needs, take care of them yourself. Don't expect your hosts to accommodate you. Thank you notes are nice after a stay with your host along with a small gift if appropriate.

You've probably seen the house rules sign in a summer beach house or mountain cottage. I think there is some old fashioned wisdom and courtesy in these rules:

Basic House Rules:

If you open it, close it.
If you turn it on, turn it off.
If you unlock it, lock it up.
If you break it, admit it.
If you can't fix it, call in someone who can.

If you borrow it, return it.
If you value it, take care of it.
If you mess it up, clean it up.
If you move it, put it back.
If it belongs to someone else, and you want to use it, get permission.
If you don't know how to operate it, leave it alone.
If it's none of your business, don't ask questions.
If it ain't broke, don't fix it.
If it will brighten someone's day, say it.
If it will tarnish someone's reputation, keep it to yourself.

Borrowing someone's car

After borrowing someone's car, you should fill the tank with gas. It would also be nice to take the car through a car wash or buy some nice thing for the car such as an air freshener or a tire gauge. If you want to be really nice, you can have the car serviced or detailed.

Travel:

Public transportation

When you ride the bus or a train, always give up your seat to the elderly or disabled. In fact, you should give up your seat to any woman regardless of age. This seems to work everywhere except New York where the women may be reluctant to take your seat. This is a cultural difference that you may not been able to overcome. Let people off the train or bus before trying to pile in. If people want to be left alone and read a book or listen to music, honor their isolation.

Airplanes

For domestic flights, stay on the lookout for people who need help finding their seat or putting their luggage in the overhead bins. Let people know when you are leaning your chair back so that you don't slam their knees or pinch their feet.

For international flights remember there are around 300 people on the plane and only a handful of bathrooms. Keep your time in the bathroom short. One time I waited 20 minutes for a bathroom. When the young man came out, he looked like he had taken a shower and the bathroom was a complete mess.

Foreign travel

We are known as the "ugly Americans" in other parts of this world. The world perceives us to be loud, aggressive, and rude. When you travel to other parts of the world, you start to understand why we have this reputation. For the most part, we tend to project that image although I hope not intentionally.

Most Americans think that the French are rude, so we have these negative expectations when we travel to France. But if you learn some rudimentary French and try to speak it wherever you go, you may be surprised. You don't have to know proper French. Preface your conversation by asking the person in French if they speak English. I tried this when I traveled to Paris, and I did not encounter any rudeness from the French people whatsoever. In fact, they were lovely people and treated me kindly.

I did see a French person be "rude" to an American. It was because the American started their encounter by speaking very loudly in English as he asked directions to the Louvre. The Frenchman simply shrugged his shoulders half way through the American's oration and left. And of course, the American said something along the lines of, "All these damn frogs are rude as hell!" Many Americans labor under the delusion that if you speak English loudly enough and slowly enough, all "foreigners" will be able to understand you. We tend to call them "foreigners" even though we are guests in their country.

I think the problem may lie in the fact that most Americans believe that everyone does or should speak English. This simply isn't true. With that attitude, most Americans approach people in other countries and start speaking English, and most of the time, their voices are loud and their tempos are slow. Try to think for a minute if a French person came up to you on the street in the USA and started speaking very loudly and very slowly in French. And when you acted as if you did not understand, he became angry and spoke even louder. When you think about it that way, perhaps you can see how the term "ugly American" came into being. It's no wonder that Americans receive rude behavior in return. So, try to learn a few phrases in the language of the country you are visiting and always ask if they speak English-in their language if possible. And if you do have to resort to English, please speak it slowly (but not too slowly), distinctly, and without volume.

Familiarize yourself with the local customs concerning methods of greeting and phrases, actions, and other things to avoid. All of the basic travel guides have this information. Avoid doing something that would be considered rude or forward. Remember this: When you are traveling to a foreign country, you are an ambassador for the United States. Please act accordingly.

There is a joke that goes something like this: What do you call someone who speaks three languages? The answer is trilingual. What do you call someone who speaks two languages? The answer is bilingual. What do you call someone who speaks one language? The answer is American. If you do nothing else, learn "please", "thank you", "sorry" and "excuse me" in the language of the countries you are visiting. Those words work their magic in any language or culture. There are thousands of websites that offer translations for these words and phrases in hundreds of different languages.

When checking into a hotel, it may speed things up if you present your passport, business card, or other identification. Saying your name may not help as your pronunciation will likely not match theirs. They will be grateful and you won't have to go through the exercise of repeating your name. Many people learn their English as British English, not US English. The pronunciations are markedly different.

The Chain of Courtesy

Because we are all connected, when we are discourteous, it can begin a chain of rudeness that can spread like a horrible virus. If one of us is late for an appointment, it not only inconveniences the person we are meeting, but it may make both of us late for our next appointment. Then we have three more people who are inconvenienced. When we are rude to someone, they may take it out on several others. These others, in turn, may be rude to more people throughout the day. This could go on for quite a while until we have a long line of angry people.

But the opposite is also true. If we are kind to people, if we are courteous and on time for our appointments, it can set off a chain of courtesy that is palpable. Remember the rampant courtesy after September 11th? That is a perfect example of this chain of courtesy.

No good deed ever goes unpunished

There will be times when you do a good deed, and it will backfire on you. This happened recently to me. I walked up to an ATM and saw a debit card sticking out of the machine. I took the card and waited for around fifteen minutes, but no one came. I called information and tried to find the person on the card to no avail. I finally called the number on the back of the card and told them the situation. They took my name and number. The next day, the woman called me and thanked me. She was from out of town and desperately needed her card. I arranged to meet her the next morning at the bank.

The next morning, she called me and said she couldn't get to the bank and wondered if I would bring the card to her. I told her I couldn't because I had a doctor's appointment that morning that could not be changed. She called me back and told me that she had arranged for someone to meet me at the bank, but asked if I could come a half hour earlier. I told her that I could. I waited for ten minutes past the time. After no one showed, I called her back and told her that I would be happy to mail her the card. I took her address and went to the doctor. During my appointment, she called eight times. Finally, I was able to answer, and her friend asked if he could come to the doctor's office and retrieve the card. I told him that he could. He came in, took the card and thanked me. Even if these frustrating things happen occasionally, don't let it discourage you from being nice and courteous.

When something good happens

When you receive good service or have a good encounter with someone, celebrate it. Tell the person's supervisor, write a thank you note to let them know that you appreciate what they have done for you. We all tend to want to report things when they go wrong. We are less likely to report when things go well.

A friend of mine was in a small diner and received very good service and a great meal cooked just the way he liked it. Before leaving, he asked to speak to the manager. "Is something wrong?", the waitress asked. "Please get me the manager", he replied. And she did. When the manager came, he extolled the virtues of his server and the cook and left a really big tip. If we celebrated our encounters with good service, we would have more and more experiences where people strive to be courteous.

When someone does something nice for you, point it out and say thank you. If someone lets you merge or turn in front of them, thank them and give them a friendly wave. Celebrate all that is good.

When all else fails

There will be times when old patterns will take over and you will become frustrated with a situation. You may have tried all the common courtesy tips to no avail. During those encounters, take a deep breath and ask yourself, is it worth the price of the anger? In the grand scheme of things, is this so important that you must get angry and raise your blood pressure and stress levels? Most of the time, the answer will be a resounding "no". So when you feel yourself starting to get angry, step back and take some deep breaths. If necessary, end the transaction, walk away, and do it another time.

Turn things around

Have you seen those individuals who are mean to others? When these mean people are in a group, the meanness seems to escalate. Couples get into the habit of being mean to each other and talking badly about each other. But you can do something about this. You can actually reverse these negative emotions. It has been clinically proven that emotions are contagious. Your attitude, whether positive or negative has a profound affect on others. Remember that the next time you see people being negative. Turn it around with your positive emotions.

Be good to one another

In this fast-paced world in which we live, we get stressed and frustrated and we tend to take it out on each other. But remember that we are all human beings and we all like to be treated nicely. That will go a long way to improve our day-to-day dealings with each other. Let us all do our best to get back that civility and gentility that we experienced during the few weeks past September 11th.

We used to greet each other by saying, "Your servant." Use this concept and submit to each other. Ask yourself, "How can I love you, serve you, accommodate myself to you?" If we do this, we will be able to bring common courtesy back into common usage. And who knows, if we take this to the extreme, perhaps we can actually save the world. Never underestimate the power of one. As the saying goes, "If everyone swept in front of their home, the whole world would be clean." It all starts with you.

 **Final thoughts**

If you think that you aren't good at developing and maintaining relationships, you are absolutely right. But I can tell you that this is a skill just like any other skill. The first thing you have to do is get your mind right. Tell yourself you are good at relationships. Practice the twelve steps. Put into practice the tenants of common courtesy. Before long, you will be a master at relationships. You will no longer feel awkward at networking meetings or large gatherings. You will feel comfortable because you possess the knowledge to cultivate relationships. Relationships drive business and personal success. Remember, relationships give you ideas, encouragement, and energy. Stop your isolation and tap into this energy. You will be glad that you did.

STRESS MANAGEMENT, TIME MANAGEMENT, AND LIFE BALANCE

By
G. Brent Darnell

 **Introduction**

Thjs book was written for tough guys. And make no mistake. The term "guy" is not gender specific. You know who you are. You are the ones who get things done. You are the alphas, the ones who make things happen, the grease that keeps things moving. You are the ones with calluses on your hands and mud on your boots. You are the tough guys. But did you know that same get-r-done attitude that you possess may be holding you back in some ways. How can that be possible?

This book is all about managing your stress, managing your time, and developing better work/life balance, an area where most tough guys fall short. First, we talk about what stress is doing to you. Then, there is a step-by-step process and practical tools to use that will reduce your reactions to the stresses in your life, give you better time management skills, and create better work/life balance. Third, there is a Body Battery Inventory and Performance Plan that will allow you to handle your stress in a positive way.

Admittedly, some of the concepts in this book may be out of your comfort zone. But I encourage you to try them. Be tough and push through your fears because if you do that,

I promise you that you will gain some benefit. This book may even save your life and prevent you from developing some horrible, stress related disease. But in order for this to benefit you, you have to keep an open mind. As the founder of Dewar's whisky said, "Minds are like parachutes. They only work when open."

Chapter 1

What is stress doing to you?
The 12 Symptoms of Stress

We live in a hectic society. We work longer hours and more days than any nation on earth. We also have the fewest paid holidays and vacation on earth. Did I sense a little swell of pride there, tough guy? I thought I did. You like to work. And there's nothing wrong with that. Stress doesn't kill anyone. We need a certain amount of stress to perform well. Stress is an every day occurrence. It's part of our lives. And for the most part, we can't control those things that are happening around us. But we do have 100% control over how we react to those situations. And it's that reaction to stress that may be killing us. Let's take a look at what stress is doing to you.

Did you know that according to the CDC, 80-90% of all illness in developed countries is stress-related? That's right, tough guy. That is what stress is doing to you. Making you sick. The USA is number one in stress-related illnesses. Hurray! We're number one! Doesn't it make you proud? Stress and burnout are epidemic. According to the American Psychological Association (APA), 75% of Americans say that work has a significant impact on their stress levels. It is estimated that US companies lose $300 billion per year in stress-related illnesses and lost productivity. That's billion with a "B".

Let's take a look at the statistics courtesy of the good old World Almanac. 80 million have cardiovascular disease. 25 million have arthritis, an auto-immune disease. That's just a fancy way of saying that the body is attacking itself. 23 million have diabetes, another auto-immune disease. And diabetes is on the rise in children and adults. It is estimated by the CDC that by 2050, almost one in three will have diabetes. 50 million have allergies and asthma. Can you say auto-immune? One in three will develop cancer in their lifetime. According to an article in Scientific American, studies show that stress hormones make it easier for malignant tumors to grow and spread. These are sobering statistics. Keep them in mind.

All of these illnesses are caused by or made worse by stress. Cardiovascular or heart disease is the number one killer in this country and around the world. In the US, one in three will die of heart disease. That includes women. Okay tough guy, I know what you're thinking. You have a genetic pre-disposition to these diseases. Yes, genetics do factor into the equation. But if you have a genetic pre-disposition to these diseases, shouldn't you be even more careful? A friend of mine, after his first heart attack, told me that he is eating anything he wants to eat because his dad died young from a heart attack and there was nothing much that he could do. Wrong!

So what about those bad habits that you have? If you smoke, tough guy, quit now. Quit as you are reading this sentence. Vow to put that cigarette down and never pick one up again. Smoking is without a doubt, one of the worst things you can do to your body. I know because my dad smoked for 50 years. He died from COPD (chronic obstructive pulmonary disease) and had terrible quality of life before his death in 2009. He was on oxygen and had chronic infections in his lungs. On one trip to the hospital for pneumonia, he caught something called pseudomonas, which is an antibiotic resistant bacterial infection that basically never goes away. He said to me, "If I thought I would have lived this long, I would have taken better care of myself."

I don't care what you have to do, quit. Do the patch, the gum, the pills, get hypnotized, but stop it now! Did you know that according to one WHO (World Health Organization) study, smokers under 40 are five times more likely to have a heart attack than non-smokers? Did you know that according to another WHO study, 80% of all people ages 35-39 who had heart attacks were smokers? Smoking in this group was judged to be the cause of 65% of all the non-fatal heart attacks in women and 55% of all of the non-fatal heart attacks in men.

Are you overweight? Obesity is another one of those epidemics that we are facing. According to the BMI (Body

Mass Index), 2/3 of adults are overweight, and half of those are obese. If you are overweight, you must take action now. We'll talk about specifics later, but make a vow right now to get that weight off and keep it off. Did you know that there is a possible link to stress and obesity? We are the most stressed nation on earth and also the fattest nation on earth. I believe that there is a correlation. Recent studies have linked cortisol, the stress hormone, with keeping weight on.

Many of you have poor eating habits with lots of frozen foods, fast food, and pre-packaged dinners. You have sedentary lifestyles. You sit a lot and watch a lot of television. You don't exercise as you should. And what is the cost? Being overweight contributes to all of these illnesses. It is the main cause for the increase in diabetes. It contributes to heart disease. It is estimated that illnesses related to obesity costs our nation $117 billion dollars per year.

So what is our nation doing about this epidemic? We have a $33 billion diet industry. Take a look at magazines and television. There is a new miracle weight loss pill out each week. We have a $20 billion cosmetics industry that covers up all of the imperfections and tries to make us look "young". We have a $300 million cosmetic surgery industry. Now, you can just go in and get the fat sucked right off. Men can now get facial reconstruction, pec implants and tummy tucks. We are obsessed with youth and thin bodies and unwrinkled faces. Everyone is looking for magic bullets and quick answers to their weight issues.

But there are no easy answers and no quick fixes. We will discuss how to deal with weight later in the book.

There is a book called *Why Zebras Don't Get Ulcers* by Robert M. Sapolsky. It's about how mammals have the fight or flight response built in. It's in the very primitive part of our brain, the limbic system. When we are faced with danger, our brains start pumping out cortisol. Our body pumps out adrenaline. The blood flows away from our middle and to our arms and legs. Our fists clench. Our jaws tighten. Our heart rate and respiration rate increase dramatically. We are ready to fight or flee.

So where do Zebras come in? All mammals have this fight or flight response. When a zebra sees a lion, its body does exactly the same thing. Since it cannot fight a lion, it prepares to run. And when the danger is over, the zebra's body goes back to normal within a short period of time. He either escapes the lion or is eaten. Either way, the danger has passed. The problem with human beings is that we experience this fight or flight response all day long.

Are you hearing me, tough guy? As human beings, when we experience stressful moments, our body acts exactly the same as if our lives were in danger. It starts the fight or flight response. It pumps out cortisol and adrenaline. It prepares us to fight or flee. So your alarm clock doesn't go off and you get a shot of adrenaline and cortisol. You walk outside and see that you have a flat tire. More adrenaline and cortisol. You are late, so you are now stuck in traffic. More adrenaline and cortisol. And this happens all day long.

How many of you have been involved in a near death experience like an accident or rescue? There is story after story about men lifting cars off people. That adrenaline rush helps us to do those kinds of superhuman things. But ask yourself or ask anyone who has been through such ordeals. How do you feel afterward? Exhausted, right? So is it any wonder that you are exhausted at the end of the day? Your body has been in fight or flight all day long. So once you hit that La-z-boy and relax, you collapse in a heap. Many people in our programs say that it is all they can do to eat dinner, spend a little time with the family, and go to bed.

Here's another phenomenon that I see quite a bit. You see, tough guy, adrenaline is a marvelous thing. It can keep you going, keep you performing, keep you from getting sick. But there is a cost. It wears your body out. How many of you get sick when you go on vacation? This is quite common for stressed out people. Because the adrenaline is flowing freely, you keep going. You keep pushing. You stay at it non-stop. But after the first few days of your vacation, especially if you don't check in at the office, your body gets the message that there is no longer a lion waiting to eat you, so it stops pumping out the adrenaline and cortisol. And when those stop, your body collapses and falls into dis-ease. That's when you get a cold. It's not very fun to have a cold and to have that big physical let down on vacation.

Some of the tough guys I work with are addicted to adrenaline. They need it. They tell me, "I love to work!" But they don't really look at the costs. Some can't get enough adrenaline at work so they take up hobbies like skydiving and bungee jumping. Okay. I want you to hear me tough guy. If you don't build in recovery for your body, you will wear your body out and die at an early age. Is that clear enough?

One other thing about adrenaline. Guess what it does to your brain? This fight or flight response comes from the limbic system. This is the primitive part of your brain and this response is for pure survival. But what it also does is shut down the neocortex or the thinking part of your brain. Because when you are being chased by a lion, it is not in your best interest to over-analyze the situation. So not only are you stressed, but your thinking brain isn't working as it should. Therefore it takes you much longer to work through any cognitive processes that you are trying to accomplish.

There is another phenomenon with this adrenaline production all day long. Because you are getting those little shots of adrenaline with each annoying thing that happens (note it is your reaction to these things, not the things, that are causing this), there is a buildup of adrenaline throughout your day. It is common that one little thing can set you off. It's like you have a cup that is almost full, and when that last little annoying thing happens such as your spouse saying something snotty or your kid leaving his toy out for you to trip over, you explode. Your cup has run over and you are out of control.

You experience what is known as an amygdala highjack. The emotional part of your brain takes over, and you go off like a rocket before the thinking part has a chance to process the information. Then you feel badly about it. It's as if you were out of your own body. Like you had no control. This is adrenaline overload, and you never know what is going to set you off.

So what is all of this stress doing to your body? You know that the long-term effect of stress is disease, but what does it do prior to the disease showing up in your body? There are physical symptoms of stress. It is your body's way of telling you that something is wrong.

These are twelve symptoms of stress:

1. Headaches

There are 40 million chronic headache sufferers in the US alone. If you have more than a couple of headaches per month, this is likely a symptom of stress. There are different kinds of headaches. There are stress headaches that start in the back of the neck and by the end of the day is a full-blown, debilitating headache. There are sinus headaches and migraines. All of these headaches are caused by or made worse by stress. Most headache sufferers accept this as normal. It is common, but far from normal. If your body is working properly, you should not be getting headaches.

2. Pain

If you have any kind of chronic pain such as back pain, joint pain, fibromyalgia, or any other kind of pain, this may be a sign of stress. People with chronic pain are usually drained at the end of the day. It takes a lot of energy to function with pain.

3. Fatigue

We talked about being exhausted at the end of the day. Some folks have Chronic Fatigue Syndrome or Yuppie Flu. If you have a hard time finding the energy to get through the day or if you are exhausted when you get home in the afternoon or evenings, this is likely a symptom of stress.

4. Difficulty sleeping

Do you have difficulty falling asleep or do you wake up in the middle of the night and find that you can't go back to sleep? Are your sleep patterns all over the place? Do you only fall asleep from exhaustion? This could be a sign of stress. Keep in mind that the CIA uses sleep deprivation as torture. Lack of sleep can cause psychosis. At the very least lack of sleep makes you less efficient and can cause other health issues.

Several of my clients have sleep apnea and require a CPAP (continuous positive airway pressure) machine in order to get a good night's sleep. They tell me that the difference in the way that they feel when they use their CPAP is like night and day. They feel so much better when they get a good night's sleep. They also tell me that when there is less stress in their lives, they are less dependent on their machine. They sleep better naturally.

5. Stomach problems

Acid stomach, Acid reflux, Chron's Disease, Irritable Bowel Syndrome, Ulcers. If your stomach isn't working as it should, if it is not performing its duty of processing and digesting food properly, it could be a sign of stress. When you are in fight or flight, your body removes the blood from your internal organs including the stomach. So if you eat while you are stressed, your stomach is unable to properly digest your food. And acid reducing medications only make things worse. Without the proper acid to digest your food, you don't get the nutrition you need. And when the body doesn't get the proper nutrition, it has to work that much harder. There is not enough fuel to do the things you need to do, and you are exhausted at the end of the day.

Did you know that most original onset of Chron's Disease immediately follows a stressful episode in a person's life? Did you know that irritable bowel syndrome is greatly helped with stress management? Stress has been shown to make all of these stomach issues worse. Recent studies have found a bacterial link to ulcers, but the studies also show that existing ulcers are more painful when the patient is experiencing emotional stress. You wolf down fast food and work through lunch in a mad race to get more done. Is it any wonder that your stomach rebels?

6. Irritability

I know. Tough guys never get irritable. But for those of you who do, for those of you who lose it when someone pulls out in front of you or a subordinate doesn't perform to your liking or someone cuts in front of you in line, this may be a physical sign of stress.

7. Problem turning off your mind

Have you ever gotten that song stuck in your head and couldn't get it out? Did you ever wake up in the middle of the night thinking about something and could not turn those thoughts off? This could be a physical sign of stress. At the very least it is a physical sign of being overwhelmed. We will discuss ways to control this later in the book.

8. Sinus problems, allergies, and asthma

Many people suffer with these physical signs of stress. These are all auto-immune maladies. It is the body attacking itself. When you think about it, there is no good reason why the body should start pumping out histamines because of dust or pollen. These substances aren't dangerous to our bodies, but our bodies react as if they were. A friend of mine is an asthma specialist. He told me that there is one thing that has reduced emergency room visits from his patients. He gave them his pager number and told them to contact him any time of day or night. Just knowing that he is there for them reduces their anxiety and stress and therefore reduces their attacks that warrant a trip to the emergency room. If you have any of these auto-immune symptoms, you may be under stress.

9. Skin problems

Rashes, hives, shingles. Most of these episodes are brought about by stressful circumstances. If you experience these symptoms, you may be under too much stress.

10. Diminished sex drive

This is a big issue for tough guys. It is a fact that the older we get, the less drive we have for sex. But stress can accelerate this process. Again, this may be common, but not normal. Healthy men should be able to have sex well into their sixties and perhaps even seventies. If you are experiencing this, you may be under too much stress.

11. High blood pressure and cholesterol

These are classic symptoms of stress. You can tell the stressed out guy with the red face who yells a lot. It's a cliché. He will likely have issues with blood pressure. It's even made it into our lexicon. We say, "Boy that sure raised my blood pressure." And stress raises cholesterol levels as well. There also may be a link between high stress and poor lifestyle habits such as diet and smoking, and these will also contribute to higher cholesterol.

12. Diminished immune response-frequent colds or flu

If you are sick a lot, you may be under too much stress. It also may be because of the adrenaline response to fight or flight. Whenever you let go and relax, over the weekend or going on vacation, your body gets sick. And your immune system is compromised, so you can't fight it off very well. If you get more than one or two colds per year, this is not normal.

So there you have it. Twelve symptoms of stress. They are your body's way of telling you that something is wrong. It's trying to get your attention. It's like a light going on in the dashboard of your car. So you're traveling down the road and a light comes on. What do you do? Do you put a piece of tape over it? You hear a loud knocking coming from under the hood. Do you turn the radio up? No. You probably take your car into a mechanic to see what is wrong and get it fixed. But your body is giving you those warning signs and what are you doing about them? You are probably ignoring them or covering them up. Most of us treat the symptom, not the underlying cause, which is the stress itself. And most of us treat our cars better than we treat our bodies.

The drug companies have figured this all out. They not only have drugs for the diseases caused by stress, they have drugs that will alleviate all of the symptoms of stress. For headaches and other kinds of pain, there are a wide variety of pain relievers and prescription drugs. The drug companies have recently come out with pills that treat combinations of these symptoms. They now have pain pills with a sleep aid that you can take at night. And in the morning, you can take a special pain pill for morning pain and stiffness.

For fatigue there are prescription drugs and over the counter remedies galore. There are dozens of "energy" drinks such as Red Bull and 5 Hour Energy to give us a boost in energy, which is usually short lived and followed by a crash. For difficulty sleeping we have Ambien, Rozerem, and Lunesta, and a variety of over the counter sleep aids. For stomach problems, we have Nexium, Protonics, Prilosec, Prevacid, Pepcid, Zantac, Reglan, Carafate, Aciphex, specific drugs for Chron's and irritable bowel, and a wide variety of over the counter antacids such as Rolaids, Maalox, Mylanta, Rennie, Pepto Bismol, and Tums.

I used to visit the shiny white first aid kit in the jobsite trailer to pop a couple of aspirin and antacids as a pre-emptive strike on my daily acid stomach and stress headache. For irritability we have a variety of anti-depressants which even out our moods. Since 2000, the use of antidepressants has doubled. Frequent colds and flu are treated with hundreds of over the counter cold medications.

There are dozens of drugs for sinus problems, allergies, and asthma. We treat most skin irritations with drugs as well. For diminished sex drive, we have Viagra and Cialis among others with shots of testosterone thrown in for good measure. There are dozens of drugs that treat high blood pressure and cholesterol, and now there is one that treats your high blood pressure and your high cholesterol at the same time.

Here is an interesting fact: our bodies need cholesterol to manufacture testosterone. When we take cholesterol lowering drugs, many times it lowers our cholesterol so that we aren't manufacturing as much testosterone. Guess what? That lowers our sex drive so that we need to take another drug.

Again, all of these drugs from that $248 billion industry treat all of the symptoms of stress, but they never address the underlying cause, which is the stress itself. We spend more than any nation on earth on healthcare, but we are one of the sickest nations on the planet. Don't get me wrong. I'm not demonizing drug companies or doctors. My niece would be dead without her daily doses of insulin. All I am saying is that doctors are trained to treat symptoms with poisons. Take a look at the inserts to these drugs. The side effects can be worse than what they are treating. And almost all of these drugs tax the liver because they are toxic. Take a look at over the counter medications. They tell us not to use them for more than a few days, but some of us take these medications every single day over long periods of time.

Doctors do what they are trained to do, treat symptoms. They are not trained to look at the root causes. What do you think the symbol for doctors means? It is the Rod of Asclepius that has a snake wrapped around a staff. The snake represents the poisons that are given to patients in the correct amount to alleviate their suffering. In this country, we take 25 tons of aspirin every single day! In 2006, there were over 2.3 billion "drug mentions" (medication that is provided, prescribed, or continued at the visit, including over the counter preparations) in the US. Many people I know who are in their fifties are on at least three or four different drugs. And when one drug causes another symptom, most doctors just prescribe another drug to treat THAT symptom. Our per capita spending on healthcare (which should be called sick care) is $7,500. The next highest country was Germany at $3,204. And we are still the sickest nation on the planet.

We live in this fix-it society. We are overworked, and we can't slow down. We don't get enough down time to stay healthy. We want a quick fix. We want to alleviate the symptoms so we can keep going. I remember in college when I was elated when they came out with Dayquil. Now I could take Nyquil at night and sleep, then take Dayquil all day to keep going, even when I was sick. Can I get a witness tough guys?

So now we see it in black and white. We are stressed and our bodies have these symptoms. It's trying to tell us to pay attention, to take some action and do something about the underlying cause, which is our reaction to the stresses in our lives. So how do we do that?

Chapter 2

How to deal with the stresses in your life. The 12 steps

So if you don't take drugs to cover up symptoms and you want to address the underlying stress that is causing these symptoms, what do you do? The answer is simple, but not easy. You have to do all of those things that you know you are supposed to do to lead a healthy life. What are the simple things you can do to turn your health around?

1.   Always eat breakfast

Many of the tough guys I work with don't eat breakfast at all. Breakfast for them is usually a cup of coffee grabbed on the run. If they do eat breakfast at all, it's usually a carbohydrate loaded breakfast sandwich that they have purchased in a fast food place or break truck. Either that or a sugar loaded donut or Danish. So what happens when you don't eat breakfast? You're telling your body to shut down your metabolism because there may not be any food coming for a while. And when you eat those carbohydrates, your blood sugar spikes, which sets you up for a crash later in the morning. I'm sure you've had those mid-morning comas where you needed more sugar and a jolt of caffeine to keep going until lunch.

2.   Eat five to six small meals per day

When you eat large meals, especially those loaded with carbohydrates, you spike your blood sugar. This is followed by a crash, and you have to spike it again. Each time, your crash is lower and you need more sugar and caffeine to recover. By the end of the day, you are exhausted. But if you eat five to six small meals a day and make sure you include some protein with each meal, your blood sugar is more stable. Protein is a slower burning fuel. You get some fluctuations in blood sugar, but you don't get those highs and lows. This blood sugar stabilization gives you more even energy throughout your day and you aren't exhausted at the end of it. Try to eat lighter as the day goes on. The saying is "eat like a king in the morning, like a prince at noon, and like a peasant in the evening."

3.   Eat foods as close to their natural state as possible

Try to minimize the processed foods that you eat. Eat organic and locally grown whenever you can, especially meat and dairy. If you can't buy organic fruits and vegetables, wash them thoroughly with a vegetable wash.

Processed foods, frozen dinners, and other convenience foods are usually stripped of nutrients, are high in sodium and calories, and are generally not good fuel for your body. Read labels and avoid products with high amounts of sugar, sodium, and fat. In fact, food companies have food scientists who create processed food using fat, sugar, and salt that tastes good and is cheap to make. If you want to be safe, try to shop on the perimeter of the grocery store and include meats, fruits, and vegetables in your diet.

Food companies are deceptive in their approach to selling food. They call these frozen food products thing like Healthy Choice and Lean Cuisine and Weight Watcher's Smart Ones. When we go to McDonald's, we know what we are getting, but when we buy something called Healthy Choice, we make the assumption that it is healthy to eat. I bought a Healthy Choice Chicken and Broccoli Alfredo meal. The front of the package said "Good Food, Good Life" and "Healthy Choice prepares meals that meet the highest quality and nutritional standards," so what do you think would be in this delightful, healthy, nutritious meal? Take a look:

Ingredients: Vegetables with Water (Peas, Broccoli, Carrots, Water), Water, Cooked Enriched Fettuccini (Water, Durum Semolina [Enriched with Niacinamide, Ferrous Sulfate (Iron), Thiamine Mononitrate, Riboflavin, Folic Acid], Egg Whites), White Meat Chicken with Binders (White Meat Chicken, Water, Modified Food Starch, Isolated Soy Protein, Rendered Chicken Fat, Dextrose, Maltodextrin, Salt, Chicken Flavor [Yeast Extract, Maltodextrin, Chicken Flavor

(Contains Xanthan Gum, Disodium Inosinate and Disodium Guanylate), Salt, Rendered Chicken Fat, Citric Acid, Natural Flavor], Soy Lecithin [Nonfat Milk, Soy Lecithin, Partially Hydrogenated Soybean Oil], Sodium Tripolyphosphate, Xanthan Gum, Flavoring), Cherries, Brown Sugar, Vanilla Crunch (Bleached Wheat Flour, Sugar, Palm Oil, Salt, Soy Lecithin, Natural and Artificial Flavors, Baking Soda), Parmesan Cheese (Part-Skim Milk, Cheese Culture, Salt, Enzymes), Cherry Juice (Contains Malic Acid), Contains 2% or Less of the Following: Alfredo Sauce Mix (Cream, Cheese Blend [Cheddar, Parmesan, Blue (Pasteurized Milk, Salt, Culture, Enzymes)], Dried Whey, Butter [Cream, Salt], Nonfat Dry Milk, Modified Cornstarch, Buttermilk, Flavor, Maltodextrin, Salt, Cultured Whey, Wheat Flour, Disodium Phosphate, Lecithin, Partially Hydrogenated Soybean Oil, Lactic Acid, Citric Acid, Tocopherol, Ascorbyl Palmitate, Ascorbic Acid), Modified Food Starch, Soybean Oil, Alfredo Cheese Blend (Parmesan, Cheddar, and Romano Cheeses [Pasteurized Cow's Milk, Cultures, Salt, Enzymes], Water, Nonfat Dry Milk, Enzymes, Disodium Phosphate, Salt, Trisodium Citrate), Whey Protein Concentrate, Salt, Chicken Broth Powder (Maltodextrin, Chicken Broth, Salt and Flavors), Garlic Powder, Onion Powder, Locust Bean Gum, Disodium Phosphate, Mono- and Diglycerides and Datem (Emulsifier), Almond Extract (Almond Oil and Other Natural Ingredients, Water and Alcohol), Spice, Alfredo Seasoning (Maltodextrin, Dextrin).

Doesn't that make you hungry? This food product is full of hidden sugars, transfats, artificial colors and flavors, and chemicals. Start reading labels and make better choices. A pretty good rule of thumb is if you can't pronounce it, you probably shouldn't eat it. That goes for hygiene products as well. Make sure your soaps, shampoos, conditioners, shaving creams, and lotions have as few chemicals as possible. These chemicals are absorbed through your skin and have to be eliminated as toxins through your liver.

4.   Minimize Fast Food and Eating Out

Take a look at the following list: college, computers, software, cars, movies, books, magazines, newspapers, music and videos. Guess what we spend more on than all of these things combined? The answer: Fast food. I like fast food. I really do. But I try to minimize my intake of fast food and use it as a treat every once in a while. Fast food tastes good. It's comfort food. I remember in college my favorite hangover meal was a cheeseburger, fries, and a coke. If you have any trouble giving up fast food, watch the films Fast Food Nation or Super Size Me. They are eye openers.

If you must eat fast food, do it in moderation. Order a salad and a small cheeseburger instead of a Super-Sized Quarter Pounder with Cheese Meal. If you must eat out, try to order things that are minimally processed and fairly nutritious. Ask the chef for healthy alternatives. Probably the best meal to eat out is sushi. It is minimally processed and contains fairly dense nutrition.

You need carbohydrates to maintain serotonin and the even mood it produces. But don't overdo the carbohydrates and always try to include some protein. Keep bars handy with a good protein/carbohydrate balance. And if you eat carbohydrates, make them complex carbohydrates, not refined sugar. Try fruit and whole grains. Avoid processed, carbohydrate loaded snacks, which are mostly just empty calories.

5.   Reduce simple sugars

Avoid processed sugars and sweets altogether and if you must have them, minimize the intake. Americans eat 150 pounds of sugar per year. Sugar has been linked to heart disease and has been shown to decrease your immune response. It's not a good thing to eat too much. Skip dessert, and if you need something sweet, go for the fruit instead. Also, keep an eye on starches like pasta, rice, and potatoes. These starches will convert directly to sugar in your body.

6.   Live to be 100!

Do you want to live a healthy life until you are 100 years old? It's possible. There was a study done of people all over the world who lived to be 100 or more. They looked at all kinds of factors such as diet, exercise, genetics, water sources, etc. What they found out is that no matter the type of diet or the lifestyle, there were three things in common: They ate 1/3 of the calories that we eat. They ate around 1,200 calories a day. The average American eats 3,600 calories per day.

The second thing is that they all had some kind of family or community support. They were not isolated. They had interaction with people on a daily basis. And the third thing was that they were thankful each day. They counted their blessings and had some kind of spiritual component to their lives. It is physiologically impossible to be stressed and thankful at the same time. Take note tough guys. If you want to live to be 100, follow this recipe.

7.   Stay hydrated

Drink plenty of water, filtered if possible. Our bodies are around 70% water. We can go approximately 70 days without eating food, but without water, we die within a week or two. Everyone needs different amounts of water, but the general rule of thumb is to drink half your weight in ounces per day. Water keeps things moving in your digestive track, it lubricates things, it keeps your brain functioning properly, it gets rid of toxins in your body. It keeps your skin healthy-the largest organ in the body. Did you know that headache is one of the first signs of dehydration? If you drink lots of water, it can also cut down on what you are eating because you will feel full. Don't drink water or other liquids while you are eating. Wait until you are finished with your meal prior to drinking and only drink a few ounces. Drink between meals if you can. This helps with your digestion. When you drink too much during a meal, you dilute the stomach acids that are vital for the first stages of digestion.

8.   Use caffeine, nicotine, and alcohol in moderation

If you can cut out nicotine altogether, that's probably best. But if you can't, cut down. Caffeine is like a whip on your nervous system. All of that coffee and all of those Red Bulls and 5-Hour Energy Drinks will keep you going, but there are consequences. There is a moment of reckoning where everything crashes. I love my coffee in the morning, so what we've done is gradually made the beans 1/2 decaffeinated and 1/2 caffeinated. This way, I can drink more coffee without the guilt. And I change to decaf in the afternoon. Some studies show that an occasional alcoholic drink can actually be good for you. But don't overdo it. A six pack every evening is probably not a good way to deal with the stresses of life.

9.   Exercise

I know. This is a tough one. But it is essential for good health and for dealing with stress. Don't over-commit. The first thing to do is to find an exercise that you love. If you try to do something that you hate, you will likely not do it on a regular basis. Yoga is a great exercise. So is swimming. Walking is also good. And this is something you can do with the family. Start slowly. Even ten minutes of walking or yoga three or four times a week will yield results. Find an exercise partner. You can hold each other accountable and make sure each of you sticks to the commitment.

10.   Quiet your mind

I cannot stress this one enough. Build in quiet time for yourself each day. Peter Senge says that everyone pursuing personal mastery practices some form of meditation each day. You have to have down time. You can call it reflection time, prayer time, meditation time, personal time, quiet time, vision time, whatever. And it doesn't have to be long. It can be ten minutes a day before the family gets up or ten minutes after they've gone to bed. Maybe you can find time to get away during the day and have that quiet time. Find what works for you. Listen to some nice music without any lyrics in order to calm your mind. Take a walk. On your commute, turn off talk radio and reflect. If you could only commit to one thing, this is it. Quiet your mind every day.

11.   Seek rest and recovery every 90 to 120 minutes

This is a tough thing for most tough guys. It's hard to stop and take a break. You want to push and push until it all gets done. But it's never done, is it? You will be much more productive if you will learn to stop and take a break and build in some kind of recovery activity every 1-1/2 to 2 hours. It doesn't have to be much. It could be some deep breathing or a walk or listening to music or a CD. Did you know that working while you are stressed and tired increases your problem solving time by up to 500%?

We do an exercise in our stress management class where half the room holds out a full soda can. These are the tough guys. They can take it. The soda can represents stress. And it's not much. They must hold the can out continuously. The other half of the room holds out their can, but they are the Zen masters. They are wise and know to take breaks. I give them short breaks where they can put the can down on the table. Then they pick them up again. After about five minutes, the tough guys are starting to strain. That little can of stress is starting to get heavy. I ask the Zen master group how long they could do this. They reply, "All day long." I then ask the tough guys how long they can do this. Many of them reply, "All day long." But they know it's not true. How many times have you pushed through your fatigue and completed something only to have to redo it the next day? Take breaks, tough guys, and get a lot more done. Check out the body battery inventory at the end of the book so that you can make a plan.

12.   Get the sleep you need

Sleep regular hours if possible. Go to bed and wake up within 1/2 hour either way each day. Everyone needs different amounts of sleep and everyone has different sleep patterns. Eight hours is a good rule of thumb. Also, naps can recharge. There was a recent study in Greece that showed that naps significantly reduced the chance of heart attacks. I used to go out to my car during lunch and grab a quick, 10 minute power nap. It made my afternoon really productive. When I was working for a contractor, I gave them the suggestion to put in a nap room, but the idea was ridiculed. But the more we learn about naps, the more we know that naps could really be beneficial for us as individuals and for companies. Are your tough guy instincts kicking in? Do you think it's wimpy to want to take a nap? Keep thinking that way. I'm sure you can take some good naps while you are recovering from your heart attack.

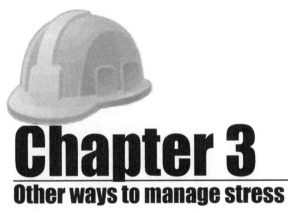

Chapter 3
Other ways to manage stress

Mindfulness

There is a way of approaching life called mindfulness. I remember seeing a cartoon in the New Yorker. Two guys are at a bar and one turns to the other and says, "Do you dwell on the wasted years behind you or the terrifying years ahead?" It's so true. Think about it. Most of our stress comes from dwelling on the past or worrying about the future. If we are completely in the moment, in the present, mindful of everything going on around us, we experience less stress. This is empirically true. There is a researcher named Jon Kabat Zinn who studies mindfulness and the effect it has on the body.

They did a study with two groups of researchers. One group was taught mindfulness techniques and learned to be fully in the moment. They were also taught proper breathing techniques. The other group did their usual work in their usual way. All measures of stress both physical and emotional showed much less stress in the group that practiced mindfulness. They had lower blood pressure, lower cortisol production, and increased DHEA, the youth hormone. It's a simple thing, but quite frankly, not easy. The fast pace of life and work causes us to get caught up in the race, and we lose the present moments. I recommend that you start with being mindful during your meals. Fully experience your meals with all of your senses. Slow down, tiger. Take your time. Chew each bite. Fully smell and taste the food. Be fully present in that moment. Then you can build on this practice and let it flow into other areas of your life.

Minimize your exposure to violent images and news

A lot of tough guys watch a lot of news, listen to a lot of talk radio, and are glued to the media. The media usually focuses on creating fear, which increases our stress levels. It's the old garbage in/garbage out theory. Minimize your exposure to those fearful and violent images, minimize the violent video games, adrenaline pumping movies, and violent stories. Stop checking the stock market ten times a day. This will decrease your stress and increase your satisfaction. Take a media break for a week and see how differently you feel. Then, you can build in media free days or weekends.

Take your vacations and holidays

Did you know that the USA is the only industrialized nation on earth without a paid leave law? Employers are not legally responsible to provide paid vacations to their employees. They only do it because they feel they must in order to attract and maintain employees. In China, if you work at the McDonald's, you get a minimum three weeks paid vacation guaranteed by the government. Americans very rarely take the full two or three weeks. And when we do, we are constantly checking our emails and answering our phones. That is not a vacation. Most of us take these days off in increments of three or four days. Long week-ends. I know, tough guy, you don't need a vacation. Many folks I work with brag that they haven't had a vacation in ten years. But what is the cost? In one study, taking a yearly vacation reduced the risk of heart attack by 30% in men and 50% in women.

European countries have anywhere from 18 to 32 days of vacation and legal holidays. We have around 16 days on average. The whole country of Sweden takes three weeks off during the summer. If you lived in Sweden, you would know why. They have long, dark, cold winters, and the summer is a time of celebration. The Swedes tell me that they need the three weeks because the first week, they are still thinking about work. The second week is a week of total decompression. The third week, they are thinking about all the things at work that they will have to do when they return.

If you want to live a long, healthy life, you must build in recovery. Vacation and time off is a way to do that. Be sure to take your vacation. Don't work every weekend. Use it as an opportunity to train people underneath you. I know this will come as a shock, but when you are gone, work goes on pretty much the same. The earth doesn't stop revolving on its axis. If you use this vacation time as a way to develop people underneath you, you will also develop the skill of delegation, which is essential to great time management.

Breathing, meditation, and yoga

We talked about being able to go for months without food and weeks without water. But you can only go for a minute or two without breathing. Breath is life. And, as adults, I think that most of us have forgotten how to properly breathe. Proper breathing is essential for good stress management. Put one hand on your upper chest and one hand below your belly button and take a deep, deep breath. Which hand moved the most? If it was the chest hand, then you have become a chest breather. That is not a natural way to breathe.

Take a look at a baby or an animal. Watch how they breathe. It's as if there whole body moves during inhalation and exhalation. As adults, we wear tight clothes, pull our belts tight, and hold our guts in. Women even resort to girdles, control top panty hose, and "slimming" pants. But what is that doing to your breathing? You probably only use the top 25% to 30% of your lungs. This reduces the oxygen in your body. Also, remember the old fight or flight response and what happens to your breathing? It gets shallow. So what you are telling your body by breathing that way is that there is a lion nearby. So your body starts pumping out cortisol and adrenaline.

In our classes, we teach full, diaphragmatic breathing. Try taking a deep breath and fill the bottom part of your lungs first. Your lower belly should rise as your breathe. Then work your way up and top off your lungs by filling your entire lungs with air. Then reverse that process. Deep breathing does all kinds of wonderful things in your body. It initiates the relaxation response, lowers your heart rate and your blood pressure. It oxygenates your brain. It makes your body function better. It reduces your stress. There is even a whole practice that involves breathing and energy called Pranajama. It takes this breathing practice to the next level.

If you want to take this relaxation response one step further, I highly encourage you to give meditation a try. Meditation is like training your brain. For those who get thoughts or songs stuck in your head and you can't get them out or wake up in the middle of the night and can't go back to sleep because you can't turn off your mind, meditation can really help. These runaway thoughts indicate that your brain is out of control. It's like a spoiled child, vying for attention. It doesn't have discipline. What if I told you that you can train your brain just like you train your body and control those thoughts?

That's where meditation comes in. And it's very simple. But it takes practice. In fact, that's what they call it, the practice of meditation. Try this simple meditation practice and see what you think. If this doesn't work for you, I encourage you to try different kinds of meditation because everyone reacts differently to these different techniques. Some people are highly visual, others aural, others are experiential. See what works best for you.

Sit in a comfortable position or lie on your back and start breathing deeply. Don't try to control your breath. Just take deep, natural, diaphragmatic breaths. Breathe in and when you breathe out, think the number one in your mind. Then breathe in and when you breathe out, think the number two. Then breathe in and breathe out and think the number three. Then breathe in and breathe out and think the number four. Then start the process over beginning with number one. Do this for three to five minutes. Set a timer if you have to.

What you will notice is that other thoughts will enter your mind and try to occupy your brain. This is your spoiled child, and you must discipline him. Don't get upset or angry about these thoughts, just politely dismiss them and go back to your breathing and counting. You will find that, at first, you will have many thoughts trying to invade your brain and take over. The yogis call this chattering monkey brain. But, over time, those thoughts will diminish, you will be in control, and you will be able to focus. This will help you when you need to focus on a task at hand or calm your thoughts in order to sleep.

There is also a great visual meditation called candle concentration. You stare at a candle for three minutes, then lightly place the palms of your hands over your closed eyes. Most of you, but not all of you, will see the negative image of the flame, much like a flashbulb ghost. Keep that image for as long as you can. You will find that it will fade and float away, but your concentration will keep bringing it back.

We teach meditation by focusing on sound as well. You can breathe and listen to a nature sound or a mantra. Focus entirely on the sound and dismiss the thoughts that float through your mind. Some people love this sound meditation and prefer it over the others.

The final meditation we teach is a guided meditation. You can purchase my guided meditation CD from the website www.brentdarnell.com. We have three music tracks and four guided meditations and visualizations. There is also a progressive relaxation where you start at your feet and work your way up your body relaxing each part as you go. For some people, these guided meditations are the best form of meditation. There are thousands of these out there. Explore them. Find one that works for you.

The more you meditate, the easier it comes to you. You will find yourself better able to focus and better able to shut off endless loops of thought. After you have gained some mastery, the next time you wake up at 1:00 in the morning and can't shut your brain off, try one of these meditation techniques. It really works once you have developed the discipline. It allows you to be more focused. This will make you more productive and efficient.

For many of these classes, we also do yoga. Now I'll admit that yoga isn't for everyone. But I highly recommend that you try it. Almost half of the participants in my classes who try yoga continue to do it. Why? Because it is so beneficial. I recently went on a yoga retreat with 35 people. I was the only man. What a great weekend!

Yoga increases lung capacity, cardiovascular function, strength, and flexibility. It reduces stress and allows your body to recover. It's low impact. It decreases injuries and joint issues. It strengthens your back. You don't need any special equipment. You can do it anywhere, even when you travel. You can purchase your own yoga mat if you want. I have purchased something called yoga paws and take them with me when I travel. Instead of taking a whole yoga mat, I take yoga paws instead. You wear them on your hands and feet, and the material is a non-slip, padded material, so you can do yoga on just about any surface without slipping. This is especially helpful in Europe where most of the floors are wood or tile.

There are a few simple forms of yoga that can be quite beneficial. There are several websites on desk yoga that will give you basic yoga moves that you can do at your desk each day. There is a very simple series of yoga moves called the Sun Salutation. Again, a simple Google search can show you these moves. The Sun Salutation stretches every muscle in your body and makes you feel great. A few rounds of Sun Salutations in the morning will make your day much better and you will have more energy at the end of the day. And it only takes a few minutes.

The Two Minute De-Stressor

We teach a quick, two minute de-stressor, which is very effective. Here are the steps:

1. Check in with how you are breathing. Is your breathing shallow? Can you help yourself by taking a few deep, diaphragmatic breaths?

2. Figure out what you are thinking. Are there thoughts that trigger these stressful episodes? If so, try to deal with those thoughts or minimize them.

3. Place the tip of your tongue on the gums just behind your front teeth. Martial artists use this technique to break boards. This is an acupuncture point that allows for energy to flow through your body.

4. Count your blessings. Think of all the things you are thankful for. It's impossible to be thankful and stressed at the same time.

Things that contribute to your exhaustion at the end of the day

There are several things that rob you of your energy. Think of your body as a battery. It's charged up in the morning, but by the end of the day, you are depleted. The first thing is to try to find ways to recharge your battery throughout the day. Build in recovery time and activities. Take breaks. Restore yourself. Secondly, is to keep an eye on the things that are depleting your battery. If you are doing activities that are robbing your energy, but not allowing you to be productive, that is a problem. I've listed the common energy robbers:

1. Nervous habits and useless movements such as tapping your feet or fingers, chewing gum or tobacco, chewing your fingernails, moving without purpose, clenching your jaws.

2. Holding muscles in tension. In yoga and meditation, we teach participants how to do a body inventory. They start at their feet and work up their bodies, trying to find areas where they are holding tension. Then they give a gentle command to those areas to relax. It takes energy to hold a muscle in tension. That drains your battery. I see many tough guys with their shoulders up around their ears by the end of the day. No wonder they are exhausted.

3. Endless loops of useless thought. It takes energy to think. And when you are thinking about non-productive thoughts and those thoughts that continue to go over and over in your mind, you are wasting energy. Meditation techniques will help you focus your thoughts, be more productive, and use less energy.

4. Being around "energy vampires." My friend, Jon Gordon, wrote a book called *The Energy Bus*. In it, he talks about energy vampires. You know who they are. Those are the people who suck the life force right out of your body. When you leave them, you feel exhausted. They

are actually feeding on your energy. Try your best to minimize your time with these people. And if you can't do that, try to find ways to recover your energy either before or after your encounters with them.

5. Not building in recovery activities and time. You must learn to take breaks and recover. Eat something, drink something, change channels mentally, get up and walk around, or listen to music. If you can develop a habit of doing this, you will be much less tired at the end of the day.

6. Not having proper nutrition. Eating foods that are nutrition dense will make you perform better mentally and physically. Good nutrition throughout your day will maintain even blood sugar levels and feed your brain and body with everything it needs to function at its best.

As we said earlier, this is one of the most difficult things you will do in your life, getting a handle on your stress and having better life balance. In the end, you do the best you can. Life will get in the way. You will get busy. But the key is checking in with yourself and getting back on track as many times as it takes. You can do it, tough guy, just like you've done all of those other things in your life.

Doing it all when you get busy

1. Exercise whenever you can. Most hotels have gyms, but you should have an exercise you can do anywhere.

I have done yoga for 30 years. It is an exercise you can do anywhere. There is a series of 12 movements called Sun Salutation. It stretches every muscle in your body, improves strength, flexibility, and cardiovascular. It also helps your organ systems to work as they should. When I have time, I do 10 rounds of Sun Salutation and add 10 pushups while I am in the plank position. In addition, for the runner's lunge, I do the warrior two pose on each side. These two additions provide excellent strength training for your arms and legs. These ten rounds take less than 20 minutes. Sometimes I just do a couple of rounds. That takes less than five minutes. You can take a yoga mat with you or purchase yoga paws, which you put on your hands and feet. The yoga paws have a pad like material that allows you to do the yoga poses without slipping. A few other exercise options are walking and working out with bands. These band workouts are easy to do and you can shove bands in your suitcase. They travel well.

2. Always wear good shoes and comfortable clothing. When you are walking through airports and traveling, it is important to be comfortable so that you can relax. A good pair of shoes makes a huge difference in the energy you expend while walking. Make sure your foot is supported and the shoes feel good on your feet.

3. Walk as much as you can. Park far away, walk instead of taking the train to the concourse when possible. If you have time, walk up and down the concourse prior to your flight. Take stairs wherever you can and find ways

to walk during your trip. When you get to the hotel, instead of turning on the television or eating, take a nice walk.

4. Invest in good luggage. I see people all of the time wearing heavy garment bags on one shoulder and a heavy computer bag on the other. This will wear you out quickly. Even backpacks, which evenly distribute the weight, can become heavy during travel. Find luggage that bears no weight on you. The best are those four-wheeled jobs that glide along with very little effort. Second to that are the two-wheeled kind. Avoid those pieces of luggage on two wheels that you have to lift off the ground. They become heavy very quickly. You would be amazed at how much energy you expend on poor luggage. Invest in good luggage and feel better at the end of your trip.

5. Eat the best food possible. Always carry food with you if possible. Take some good bars with some protein, some good fruit or nuts or other healthy snack. Most plane food is carbohydrate loaded. Make sure you have some protein to mix with it. Probably the best choice if you have to eat out is sushi. It has the least amount of processing. If you have to eat fast food, try a salad and a small burger or sandwich instead of the Quarter Pounder with Cheese Supersize Meal.

6. Stay hydrated. Drink plenty of water and avoid caffeine, especially when you are on airplanes. When you arrive, take a quick shower to rehydrate your skin.

Involve the Entire Family

Several participants have brought their whole family in on the process of being better and getting healthier in something they call the eight-week family makeover. The family agrees on the things they are trying to accomplish together as a family such as exercising more, watching less television, playing less video games, eating healthier meals, losing weight, quitting bad habits, etc. The family keeps a log for each member on how they have done on these agreed upon initiatives. There can be prizes for the family members who accomplish the most. This is a great way for the family to support each other in this healthy endeavor. And most of the time, these habits last beyond the eight weeks.

Ignoring stress has its consequences

I worked with a person who was very driven, a typical type "A" personality in his mid-thirties. He was placed as a project manager on a very difficult project. There was a huge penalty for not finishing the project on time, and there was a lot of pressure. My friend worked ungodly hours for months on end. Then, one day, he started developing something called cluster headaches. These headaches are some of the worst kind that you can get. The people who experience them say it's like having a hot poker thrust through your eye. Drugs are not very effective. They call them cluster headaches because they come on like clockwork.

My friend needed to keep working, so he went to the doctor to try and find some relief. He never thought about slowing down his work schedule or taking some time off. The doctor prescribed Prednisone, a steroid. He would start off with a large dose, then gradually diminish the dose each day. This, the doctor said, would get rid of the headaches. My friend took the first dose and went to bed. The next day, he had severe pain in his hip joints. He couldn't get out of bed. He went to the hospital and was diagnosed with aseptic necrosis in his hip joints, which meant that the hip bone was dead. He was now faced with hip replacement surgery and the possibility of being disabled.

He has learned to cope with this situation. He tried some vascular surgery to help the bone, but it was not successful. He is now in constant pain. The question that keeps going over and over in my mind is what if he had stopped working and addressed his stress levels? Would this have even happened to him? I can't say. But I do know that health issues for men in their forties and fifties can be life altering. How many people do you know that are having heart attacks and the onset of diseases like diabetes and arthritis? Don't be a victim. Take responsibility for your health right now. This very moment. Don't let your tough guy attitudes lead you to an early grave. Pay attention or face some pretty dire consequences. And if you aren't willing to do it for you, then do it for your family. They probably want you around for a long time.

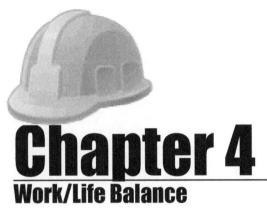

Chapter 4
Work/Life Balance

saw a cartoon once with a man and his family sitting around a table. The caption reads "Before we begin our family meeting, how about we go around and say our names and a little something about ourselves." One participant told me that he was commuting once a week and sometimes every other week. One week, he came home, and his two-year old daughter was afraid of him. She didn't know who he was. That was a big wake up call for him. He vowed to get home more often.

Have you noticed something about those really successful guys? They seem to have pretty good work/life balance. Now, they may have sacrificed that balance at times in their careers. That's understandable. But they have learned valuable lessons. They have learned what the true definition of success is. And it's not working your ass off until you have a heart attack at age fifty.

What is your work/life ratio? Ideally, the ratios should go something like this: 33% work, 33% family, and 33%

personal. For most of us, it's 70-80% work, 10-20% family, and 0-10% personal. I don't know of anyone who has reached this ideal, but it's something to keep in your mind. Most tough guys sacrifice themselves first. This isn't a very good strategy because if you don't take care of yourself, you're no good to your employer or your family. So the first thing to do for good work/life balance is to schedule more time for you.

Who suffers when your life is out of balance? I'm sure there is some personal suffering, but the family also suffers. I know, tough guy, you work really hard because you love your family and you want to provide for them. But ask them what they would rather have. I think you know the answer. No one has ever said on their deathbed that they wish they could have worked a little more and spent less time with their families. My classes are filled with older tough guys who have real regrets over not spending more time with family, especially their children. Tough guys take note. Don't be full of regret at the end of your life and career. Start working toward better work/life balance.

Don't get me wrong. It's not easy. This is probably one of the hardest things you will ever do. But the payoff is tremendous. And the smart employers want you to have good work/life balance as well. They want you making money for them for a long time, not just until your health fails from burnout.

The next chapter is about time management. If you manage your time better, you will have more time for yourself and your family.

Chapter 5
Time Management

Time management has nothing to do with managing your time. It's about managing yourself. And the main reason people don't manage themselves well is that they get on other people's agendas. They allow others to manage their time for them. It's time you took control and managed yourself.

We use a little different approach to time management. Because I work with a lot of construction guys, we take the same approach as creating a schedule for a project. There are simple steps:

1. When is the end? When is the project to be completed? What is the end date? You must know when the client expects his building. It's no different with your life. What is your end date? When will you be done? By "done", I mean dead. Now none of us know exactly when we're going to die, but we can look at statistics and get pretty close. Think about it. You have around 4,000 weeks on this planet. You probably have around

2,000 left. What are you going to do with those 2,000 weeks?

2. Lay out the mission. What are your general philosophies for your project (your life)? Many projects write down their mission or general plan for the project. They go something like this: "Our mission is to build a quality project on time, within the budget, with zero accidents and zero defects." So what should go in your mission statement? I'll share mine with you: "To make the world a better place. To make a positive difference in people's lives the world over and help them to develop their potential in order to change their lives for the better. To work until I'm 90 and grow old gracefully alongside my wife. To create massive wealth and give most of it back to family, friends, my community, and the world."

3. Set your milestones. What are your milestones? What are the major things you want to do or accomplish before you die? Write these milestones down. It might be specific goals or general things. Pay for the kids college, learn a language, become a great dad or husband, build a mountain home, attend church more, start another career, travel more, work less. What are those milestones? Be sure to write them down. Make a list. Keep in mind all of the different hats that you wear in life and you may have some milestone goals for each of those.

4. Make a schedule. Once you have all of this preliminary

work done, you must start on your actual schedule. You have things that you want to accomplish. You have an end date. Now what activities must you schedule to attain all of your goals? Contractors do this very practically. If they have 1,000 pieces of precast to set in 100 days, they know they must set 10 pieces per day to reach that goal. If you want to learn a language, you must schedule a class or time to work through language tapes. If you want to pay for your kids' college, you must make a budget and set aside money each month. If you want to become a better husband, you must schedule dates and time with your wife. Those things don't just happen. You have to schedule activities that propel you toward those goals. Daily schedules don't work as well for the day-to-day work things that pop up all day long. This time management method simply does not work any longer. But schedule the things that are important to you. Schedule the things that you value. In addition, try scheduling your week like a four-day work week. Try not to schedule anything on Fridays. This may not work for some weeks, but for most weeks, this is probably feasible. That way, you can use Fridays as your overflow day, your catch-up day, so that just maybe you will avoid coming in on some Saturdays.

5. Work your plan. Once you have your schedule, you must work your plan. This takes discipline and accountability. Find that accountability in your spouse a good friend, or a support group. However you need to do it, do it. Without the accountability, this is all for naught. Make this happen. Stephen Pressfield says,

"Never forget: This very moment, we can change our lives. There never was a moment, and never will be, when we are without the power to alter our destiny. This second, we can turn the tables on resistance. This second, we can sit down and do our work."

6. Find out how you are spending your time right now. Do a time log for a week. How do you spend a typical week? Write down everything you do and how you are spending every minute of every day for a week. At the end of the week, review how you are spending your time. Are you doing the activities that are propelling you toward your goals? Or are you doing a lot of activities that are wasting a lot of your time? When I did this, it was a real eye opener. I have my own business, and when I did my time log, I found out I was spending 60% of my time doing administrative crap. I was spending most of my time doing things that made me no money. So the next day, I hired an administrative assistant and gave her all of that stuff to do. It's made a tremendous difference.

My wife and I now say, "If it doesn't bring us joy or make us money, we will try to get someone else to do it." We are really into outsourcing our lives. We outsource work tasks, the cleaning of the house and the maintenance of the yard. The other day, she asked me to order some glass so that she could reframe a picture. I dropped the picture off and told the frame shop to do it.

7. The four immutable rules of time management. Note, some of these concepts are from David Allen's book, Getting Things Done, which I highly recommend.

   a. Empty your head. Get everything out of your head and onto pieces of paper. Use one piece of paper for each thing. When I did this, I had a stack of papers a foot high. Martial artists use this concept. They empty their mind and focus so that they are ready for anything. When you have a million things on your mind, you can't have good time management.

   b. Put these things in a system that you like. There are several good systems out there. Put it into a system where you know it won't get lost. David Allen has a great work flow chart if you need some ideas.

   c. According to David Allen, you should use outcome thinking. What outcome do you want? The next question is what next physical action do I need to take to propel that thing toward that outcome? This is a very important distinction. I changed from "to do" lists which seemed to just repeat to a "next actions" list with a focus on outcome thinking per David Allen. It has made a huge difference.

   d. You must review your system at least once a week. Go through everything and take items off that have been completed. Update everything with a detailed review. I try to do mine on Monday mornings.

Chapter 6
Time Wasters

1.   Lack of delegation. This is one of the biggest time wasters in business. We tough guys think that we are the only ones who know how to do things properly, so we end up doing a lot of the work ourselves. This is great for the ego, but terrible for time management. Also, this is the biggest stumbling block to getting to the next level of your career. What you should be doing is developing five of you underneath you. Those are the people who get promoted. Do you get caught up in all of those little things that don't get you big returns? Have you trained your people that they can dump problems on you and you will step up and solve them? You are allowing them to let you solve their problems for them. Again, this is very good for the ego, but not very good for time management. There are lots of reasons we don't delegate:

   a. Fear of losing control. This is a big issue with a lot of tough guys.

   b. Thinking you can do it better.

c. Fear that they may do it better.

d. Fear of overburdening staff. This is pretty silly. One guy told me that he worked most Saturdays because his staff had families. I asked him if he had a family. After a pause, he said, "Yes." Duh.

e. Inexperience with delegating. This takes practice.

f. Insecurity.

g. Being suspicious.

h. Lacking trust.

i. Being too busy. I hear this one often. By the time I explain how to do it, I could just do it myself. Sure. That time. But think of it as an investment in time. The next time that same situation comes up, that person will be able to do it and you can spend your time doing other things.

Start thinking like a CEO. They spend 30% of their time creating the vision, 30% of the time re-evaluating, 30% of their time developing others, and 10% of their time with those little things that clog up their day.

2.   Meetings can be a huge time waster. One quote I saw said, "When I die, I hope it's in a meeting. The transition from life to death will be barely perceptible." So how can you make meetings more efficient?

a. Prepare. Don't walk into meetings without preparation. Know what is to be accomplished.

b. Don't forget the food. This not only improves attendance, but keeps people's brains full of nutrition so they can think. Try complex carbohydrates instead of donuts.

c. Have an agenda. If you can't make an agenda or you don't have one, don't have a meeting. In my opinion, meetings over one hour are a waste of time and energy. Your agenda can be a timed agenda as well. Allocate certain time slots for certain topics. And stick to it.

d. Have a Timekeeper and Facilitator. This can be the same person, but you must have someone that makes sure the agenda is followed. Cut down on the rabbit trails and the personal stuff. If items come up during the meeting that are important, but not part of that meeting, put it in a parking lot. Assign someone to follow up and set up a future meeting if necessary to address it.

e. Begin on time. One time I asked this person why he was always late for meetings and he said, "We never start on time anyway." If you begin on time, people will get the message.

f. Have etiquette rules. Don't have everyone talk at once. Raise your hand to speak. No mobile phones.

g. Involve everyone.

h. End on time.

You can play a game called Bullcrap Bingo. This usually engages everyone. Create a 5 X 5 grid and write down all of those buzz phrases for meetings for your industry in each square: things such as win-win, sports analogies, synergy, think outside the box, revisit, out of the loop, proactive. During the meeting, if you hear one of these phrases, mark it off. When you have all the squares filled across, up and down, or diagonally, you yell, "BULLCRAP!" It's probably not good for a client meeting, but for an internal meeting, it can be great fun. And it gets people to pay attention.

3.　　　Phone calls. This is a big time waster. But I have found a secret that not many tough guys know. There are actually OFF buttons on these phones and Blackberrys. I'm serious. Now all you have to do is turn them off. There are times when you should turn them off. During vacations and holidays for instance. But there are other times during the day when you could silence them. When you really need to focus and get some things done, turn the darned thing off!

You can batch your calls and return all of the messages. And since you are likely to get voice mail and get put on hold, you can be checking emails at the same time. I worked with a company that had the policy that the phones were to be on 24/7. This was because they wanted to give great customer service. I question the logic of this. One guy answered his phone five times during an hour long meeting that we were having. This may be good for customer service, but horrible for time management.

4.   Emails are a real problem. Email has become a chat room, and people expect an immediate response. People can receive hundreds, sometimes thousands of emails each day. The expectation from others is that you are sitting there waiting to see their email and answer it immediately. So it is up to you to create a different expectation.

The first thing you need to do is turn off that bell that dings when an email hits. Don't you feel compelled to open it and read it? Have you become a Pavolv's dog to email? Do you salivate as well? Again, don't answer emails as they come in. Turn off your Outlook and do other things. Answer your emails in batches. And if your company doesn't have email rules to cut down on the crap, talk them into it. No personal emails with baby announcements and birthdays.

Never check your email first thing in the morning. Always start with the important things that you must accomplish. How many times have you started with emails first thing and you look up and it's noon. Resist that temptation to check emails first thing in the morning. That way, you won't wind up on everyone else's agenda.

There was a fantastic idea from The *4-Hour Work Week* by Tim Farriss. I tried it and it really works. If you want to reduce the email in your inbox by 50%, do the following: First, send out an auto-responder for a few weeks that says that in order to serve your clients better, you will only check your email twice per day, at noon and at 5:00 pm. Tell them if they really need to get in touch with you, please call your mobile phone.

If you have key clients or personnel, call them directly and let them know what you are doing. You created an expectation of immediate response. This is a process to create a different expectation.

In addition to this, create rules for all incoming emails. You can automatically send emails to subordinates from certain people and let them handle it. For those emails that you like to read, but aren't critical, put them into a read file. When you get busy, you can delete these without even looking at them.

There was a project manager that said he could never do this. He said he had to look at every email on the project. I told him that would be great for keeping an eye on things, but horrible for time management. Then, his child became ill and he travelled with him to a hospital out of state. While he was there, he couldn't check emails very often, so he tried the auto-responder. It worked like a charm and he reduced his emails by 40%. And the project didn't fall apart.

Also, I have a few email rules that make emails faster and easier to read. First, put something interesting in the subject line, maybe even the whole email. That way people won't even have to open it. Make it clear when no reply is needed. Don't send one word "thanks" emails. Don't write an email that you have to scroll down to read. Keep them short and sweet. Nobody reads those thirty page emails.

Don't add any attachments unless expected or warranted. No one opens attachments.

One other issue for email are those annoying threads that can be 20 emails long. One of our participants told us how they handle these. When the email gets to the third thread, that person is responsible for resolving the situation. They can't extend the thread, but they have to resolve it and send out a resolution emails to all interested parties.

5.   Drop in visitors. We've all heard it. Have you got a minute? But is it ever a minute? When someone says this, first, ask them what this is about. Then tell them how much time you can give them and stick to it. Or tell them that you don't have time right now. This is a great approach. Tell them you don't have time and that they should try and figure this out themselves. Tell them if they can't figure it out by 4:00 today, to come back and you will help. 90% of the time, they never come back.

If they don't get the message to leave, stand up and walk toward the door. Try putting no chairs in your office. That will keep people from staying so long. Have you seen the guy who comes in, sits down, and puts his feet up only to talk about his personal life for an hour? You can also have designated office hours for drop-in visitors. The last resort is to hide so that no one knows you are in your office.

6.   Personal clutter. Are you holding on to things that don't help you attain your goals? Does it take you a long time to find things in your office? If your house or office burned down, what would be irreplaceable? We hold on

to way too much stuff. We are in the electronic age and most of our documents aren't paper. Yet we sill experience clutter. There are some schools of thought on organization that say you should only handle a piece of paper once. David Allen, the author of *Getting Things Done*, says that if something takes less than two minutes, you should just do it. Do a de-clutter day once a week or once a month and if you haven't touched something in a month, throw it away. One person told me that they throw their paper away in a recycling box so that if they needed it later, they can always go back through the recycling.

7.   Procrastination. Do you put things off? Is this an issue for you? Most people put things off for two reasons: either they hate to do this thing or they are not good at this thing. If you're not good at something, get the training to be good at it. If you don't like doing something, try doing it first thing in the morning. When you have accomplished that thing that you hate to do, the rest of the day feels like a vacation. You can do easy hard or hard easy. Start with those difficult tasks that you hate first, then the other things will be so much easier. If you save those big things for the end, they tend to never get done.

8.   Just say no. Learn how to say no. Set limits. I know this is hard for all of those get-r-done tough guys, but you have to learn to say no. Or as my wife says, "I just can't say yes to that at this time."

9.   Idle talk and gossip. I know tough guy, you will probably tell me that you don't do this. But I don't believe

you. How many trash talk sessions do you have per day. How many bull sessions are on your agenda? These sessions can be fun and useful for relationship building, but they are horrible for time management. They waste a lot of time. Don't do it.

10.   Television and other major time wasters. Television is probably the biggest time waster on the planet. In the USA, we watch 4-1/2 hours of television per day on average. I watch an average of one hour per day, so someone out there is watching eight hours of television per day. And for those of you who say you watch less than 4-1/2 hours per day, think about ballgames, car races, ESPN, and Sports Center. With that average of 4-1/2 hours per day, by the age of 65, you've watched 12 years of television. Imagine what you could do with those twelve years. Let's add commute time (The Atlanta average is 48 minutes per day. Your commute time may be longer.), internet surfing, calls, other "wasted" time (2 hours per day). Without even figuring in holidays, weekends, and vacations, you "waste" 107 full 24 hour days each year on these kinds of activities.

What if you took ½ that time or 53 full 24 hour days and used it for yourself and your family. Which would bring you greater happiness at the end of the year? Do you sit in your car during a commute when you could be listening to some book on tape that will help you? Or some nice music? Or use that as productive, reflective time? The time is there if you just utilize it in a better way.

There will be three challenges that you will face when you start to pay attention to life balance and time management. The first is guilt. You will feel guilty when you start working less hours. But the great feeling you get by spending more time with your family will offset this guilt. The second thing is misunderstandings from others. They may think that you are becoming a slacker. They may ridicule you in your new approach. This is to be expected. They probably are going down a bad road themselves and want to take you with them. Don't let them.

The construction industry is the only industry I know where you can work 80-hour weeks for six months and when you decide to take off a Friday afternoon to see your kid's ballgame, your boss gives you grief, looks at his watch, and says, "Boy, I wish I could keep those banker's hours like you." It's insane. The third thing you might experience is painful insights. You may find that you aren't a very good husband. You may find that you are a video junkie as I did. These insights are just ways to grow. Embrace them and overcome them.

 **Body Battery Inventory & Plan**

Many stress management seminars talk about reducing the stress in your life. I'm sure there is something to that. But work and life can be very stressful. We take a slightly different approach. Imagine that your body is a battery. There is stress and other things that discharge your body battery and deplete your energy. Those things will always be there. There are also things you can do to recharge your body battery and replenish that energy. So, do your best to decrease the things that are depleting you and increase things that recharge your battery. Try to adjust how you react to stressful situations. If you can build in more ways to recharge your body battery throughout your day, you will have much more energy and be much less stressed at the end of the day.

Fill out the following body battery inventory & plan and see where you are.

Physical Symptoms of Stress and Stress Related Illnesses: Check all that apply to you. These discharge your body battery and deplete your energy.

❑ Headaches: 40 million chronic sufferers

❑ Pain-back, joint, chronic, Fibromyalgia

❑ Fatigue: exhausted at the end of the day, tired when you wake up in the morning, Chronic Fatigue Syndrome

❑ Difficulty sleeping: difficulty asleep or waking up and can't get back to sleep

❑ Stomach Problems: Acid Stomach, Acid Reflux, Ulcers, Chron's, Irritable Bowel, constipation, diarrhea

❑ Irritability, feeling on the edge, explosive nature, chest pains

❑ Allergies, Asthma, sinus problems

❑ Skin problems (dry skin, eczema, psoriasis, rashes, hives, shingles)

❑ Depression or anxiety: melancholy, no drive, or anxious feelings

❑ Frequent illness, frequent colds or flu, diminished immunity

❑ Cognitive impairment: can't think clearly, memory issues

❑ Diminished sex drive

❑ Diabetes

❑ Arthritis

❑ High Blood Pressure

❑ High Cholesterol

❑ Any autoimmune disease not listed such as lupus, pancreatitis, or MS

Total number of stress related illnesses and symptoms:_____

Things that discharge your body battery:

Work Stress:

0	1	2	3	4
none	some	moderate	a lot	insane

Personal Stress:

0	1	2	3	4
none	some	moderate	a lot	insane

Emotional Stress:

0	1	2	3	4
none	some	moderate	a lot	insane

Travel/commute stress:

0	1	2	3	4
none	some	moderate	a lot	insane

Physical Stress like training or exercise:

0	1	2	3	4
none	some	moderate	a lot	insane

Family Stress:

0	1	2	3	4
none	some	moderate	a lot	insane

Health stress (colds, illness, fatigue, etc):

0	1	2	3	4
none	some	moderate	a lot	insane

I use nicotine:

0	1	2	3	4
none	1-5 cigs	5-10 cigs	10-15 cigs	over 15

I drink alcohol:

0	1	2	3	4
none	1 drink/wk	2drink/wk	3drink/wk	4drink/wk

I am overweight by:

0	1	2	3	4
0 lbs	5 lbs	10 lbs	15 lbs	over 15

I have stress related symptoms or illness *(from pages 86-87)*:
(NOTE: Whatever you choose, you must multiply the number by 4)

0	1	2	3	4
0	1	2	3	4 or more

(Whatever you chose for stress-related symptoms or illness, multiply it by 4. So if you chose 4 (4 or more symptoms or illness), your value should be 16.) **Total on stress-related symptoms or illness:** _____

If you have had a major life shift or transition in the past twelve months (death of a loved one, a physical move, a new job, being let go from a job, bankruptcy, a failed endeavor, graduation, life-threatening illness, marriage, divorce, a new baby, or any other major life transition or major life stress), add 15 points.

Add up the total points. This is your Body Battery Discharge Number: _____

Things that recharge your body battery:

I sleep well and awake refreshed:

0	1	2	3	4
none	rarely	sometimes	mostly	all the time

I take naps or have complete downtime daily:

0	1	2	3	4
none	rarely	sometimes	mostly	all the time

I have passive recovery times daily

[reading (no news or violence), television (no news or violence), movies (no violence or upsetting movies), video games (no violence or upsetting images), music (hopefully soothing and relaxing), radio(no talk radio, news, or violence)]:

0	1	2	3	4
none	rarely	sometimes	mostly	all the time

I do relaxation exercises for recovery daily:
(meditation, yoga, breathing, massage)

0	1	2	3	4
none	rarely	sometimes	mostly	all the time

My diet is filled with nutritious foods and limited simple sugars:

0	1	2	3	4
none	rarely	sometimes	mostly	all the time

My diet is many small meals spread throughout the day:

0	1	2	3	4
none	rarely	sometimes	mostly	all the time

I eat only around 1,500 to 2,000 calories per day:

0	1	2	3	4
none	rarely	sometimes	mostly	all the time

My day has fun in it every day:

0	1	2	3	4
none	rarely	sometimes	mostly	all the time

I have at least one hour of personal time just for me each day:

0	1	2	3	4
none	rarely	sometimes	mostly	all the time

I find time for reflection (prayer, meditation, quiet time) each day:

0	1	2	3	4
none	rarely	sometimes	mostly	all the time

I connect with family, friends, and community daily:

0	1	2	3	4
none	rarely	sometimes	mostly	all the time

I am grateful and thankful each day:

0	1	2	3	4
none	rarely	sometimes	mostly	all the time

I take my full two weeks of vacation without checking in at the office:

0	1	2	3	4
none	rarely	sometimes	mostly	all the time

I have down time every weekend without checking in at the office:

0	1	2	3	4
none	rarely	sometimes	mostly	all the time

I am positive each day:

0	1	2	3	4
none	rarely	sometimes	mostly	all the time

I seek rest and recovery every 90 to 120 minutes:

0	1	2	3	4
none	rarely	sometimes	mostly	all the time

Add up the total points. This is your Body Battery Recharge Number: _____

Body Battery Recharge Number minus Body Battery Discharge Number = _____

If this is positive, keep up the good work. If it is negative or nearly equal, it is recommended that you either find more ways to reduce your body battery discharges or find more ways to recharge your body battery.

Body Battery Performance Plan

See the following page for your body battery performance plan. You likely have battery dischargers that deplete your body battery: things such as a daily commute, a daily or weekly meeting, weekly or monthly travel, an annual report, tax time, monthly progress or accounting, bill paying time, stressful family gatherings, encounters with difficult people, etc. They may be daily dischargers or occasional dischargers.

Put down the activities that are discharging your body battery and depleting your energy, then fill out what recharging activities you will do before, during, or after to recharge your body battery.

Daily body battery dischargers	Recharging activities
Occasional body battery dischargers	Recharging activities

Body Battery Recharging Activities

❑ Take five deep breaths.
❑ Think of something you are grateful and thankful for.
❑ Drink water.
❑ Do something silly. Make a face or stick out your tongue.
❑ Start a laugh club and laugh daily.
❑ Put Scotch tape on your face and distort it.
❑ Play hopscotch on the sidewalk.
❑ Play a game with kids.
❑ Do something extremely physical.
❑ Go to an amusement park.
❑ Yell at the top of your lungs.
❑ Sing or hum a song.
❑ Smile. It creates physiological changes.
❑ Take a nap.
❑ Spend some time with your pet.
❑ Go make someone's day with a surprise visit.
❑ Change your body.
❑ Throw your shoulders back.
❑ Stretch your arms over your head, then touch your toes.
❑ Plant your feet firmly on the ground. Feel the heaviness.
❑ Feel yourself as you become assertive and powerful.
❑ Turn your negative self-talk around.
❑ Create a mantra and repeat it.
❑ Visualize yourself being relaxed, calm, and full of energy.
❑ Dance around the room.

- ❑ Go to a different place physically.
- ❑ Workout with weights or do something that gets your heart rate up.
- ❑ Shake all over like a dog.
- ❑ Get some protein either in shake or in bar form.
- ❑ Go for a walk in nature.
- ❑ Call someone who is supportive and talk to them.
- ❑ Look at cool videos or your mind movie.
- ❑ Ask for a hug.
- ❑ Zone out with music.
- ❑ Watch a sitcom or stand-up comedy show.
- ❑ Take an acting class, a dance class, or an aerobics class.
- ❑ Get a massage, acupuncture, reflexology or Reiki.
- ❑ Take an improvisation class.
- ❑ Play a nonsense song on the musical instrument of your choice even if you can't play a musical instrument.
- ❑ Tell a joke.
- ❑ Open a window and get some fresh air.
- ❑ Go to some funny websites with jokes or funny videos.
- ❑ Look at a photo of someone you love.
- ❑ Explore your feelings.
- ❑ Doodle, draw a picture.
- ❑ Do the two minute de-stressor: Notice your breath. How are you breathing? Breathe deeply. What are you thinking? Are there thoughts that cause this stress? Think of things you are grateful and thankful for. Tap the tip of your tongue on the gums just above the top front teeth.
- ❑ Read a kid's book.

- ❑ Look at fish in an aquarium.
- ❑ Look at birds, squirrels and other animals near your house.
- ❑ Look under a rock and observe what is there.
- ❑ Go to a museum or aquarium.
- ❑ Help someone in need.
- ❑ Visit an assisted living place and sing a song for the residents.
- ❑ Have lunch at Chucky Cheese or other kid's restaurant.
- ❑ Have a mindful meal that lasts at least one hour.
- ❑ Make faces in the mirror.
- ❑ Give yourself a massage on your shoulders and face.
- ❑ Take a Jacuzzi.
- ❑ Run as fast as you can.
- ❑ Try to not think about zebras.
- ❑ Put on some disco and do the robot.
- ❑ Pretend to be someone else.
- ❑ Make weird noises.
- ❑ Do a puzzle.
- ❑ Make a prank phone call.
- ❑ Eat an ice cream cone or frozen yogurt.
- ❑ Get a mani pedi (that's a manicure and pedicure).
- ❑ Gargle sing a song or burp the alphabet.

Biography and Contact Information

Brent Darnell is a leading authority on emotional intelligence and is a pioneer of its use in the construction industry. Brent has helped to improve the social competence of thousands of people working with over 70 companies in more than 15 countries around the world. There is constant demand for him to deliver speeches and train others using his comprehensive and unique approach that leads to lasting behavioral transformation.

An engineer, author, actor, playwright, and musician, Darnell gives presentations that are insightful, perceptive, and wildly entertaining. The construction industry has embraced his work, and many top companies like Clark, Granite, Kiewit, Caddell, Batson Cook, Brasfield & Gorrie, INPO, S&ME, Langan Engineers, Geotechnical Services, Inc, Pinkerton & Laws, Randall Paulson, Manhattan, Lyles, Newcomb & Boyd, Guarantee Electric, Hardin, McCarthy, Heery, Jacobsen, Cousins Properties, WS Nielsen, Balfour Beatty, and Skanska, have utilized his methods for their managers. He has also worked with the CMAA, the DBIA, ASFE, the Associated General Contractors, and the Associated Builders and Contractors. In addition, he is an adjunct professor at Penn State and Auburn, teaching people skills to their technical students.

218 Stress Management, Time Management and Life Balance

Brent believes a person's emotional intelligence is one of the most important predictors of ultimate success for individuals and companies, and his proven program creates fundamental behavioral shifts in employees, improving their performance and increasing the company's bottom line. Brent is a graduate of the Georgia Institute of Technology, and lives in Atlanta, GA with his wife Andrea and their dog Ginger.

If you wish to contact Brent Darnell concerning this emotional intelligence work, please visit _www.brentdarnell.com_. Also check out the Total Leadership Program website at www.totalleadershipprogram.com .

You may also email him at _brent@brentdarnell.com_
or drop him a line at
Post Office Box 13064
Atlanta, GA 30324 USA